Dear, Marsha,

Treasure each day,
live it with faith,
joy — & our memories —
be beautiful.

Matilda Balao

LEAD ME, GUIDE ME

The Spiritual Rapture of Heaven

By Matilda Balas

Copyright © 2007 by Matilda Balas

ISBN 0-7414-3827-5

Cover design by Darnesha Walker

Edited by Eilene Balas and Reaitta Irby

Published by:

INFI∞ITY
PUBLISHING.COM

1094 New DeHaven Street, Suite 100
West Conshohocken, PA 19428-2713
Info@buybooksontheweb.com
www.buybooksontheweb.com
Toll-free (877) BUY BOOK
Local Phone (610) 941-9999
Fax (610) 941-9959

Printed in the United States of America

Printed on Recycled Paper

Published May 2007

Dedication

In loving memory of my beloved son
George David Balas
whose death inspired me to write this book.

"Behold the fowls of the air; for they sow not, neither do they reap, nor gather into barns; yet your heavenly Father feedeth them. Are ye not much better than they?"

(Matthew 26:28, KJV)

"Take therefore no thought for the morrow; for the morrow shall take thought for the things of itself. Sufficient unto the day is the evil thereof."

(Matthew 26:34)

Ronnie, Leslie, and Robert remember their carefree days of childhood, growing up together with their brother George. The bond of love that kept them together from childhood through adulthood was strong and meaningful, and is now everlasting.

Acknowledgments

I wish to thank my wonderful friends for the time, dedication, and spiritual knowledge they gave to the writing of this book.

My heartfelt thanks go to Reverend Frank Shepherd for writing the foreword. He was an exceptional pianist and a graduate of the Juilliard School of Music; he gave up his music to pursue his calling to the ministry. For the past fifty years, he has devoted his life to helping others. He has been the pastor of several Hungarian/American churches in the Cleveland, Ohio, area. In my conversations with Reverend Shepherd, he has always been inspirational. I am grateful to have his spiritual knowledge added to my book.

After I began writing, I knew I needed a computer. I contacted my dear friend Reaitta Irby. I felt she could help me. After she read a couple of pages she said, "Finish the book. This is awesome." Reaitta took on the project of computerizing the manuscript, revising, and editing. Reaitta is deeply involved with helping others and devotes much of her time to ministry. Her spirituality and knowledge of the Bible has truly been a blessing in the writing of this book.

Eilene Balas is my daughter-in-law. She is a wonderful person who shared her life and dreams with my son George. She spent many hours reading and editing the manuscript. Once again she relived the past, and shed tears remembering the love and laughter they had together.

My sincere gratitude goes to Darnesha Walker for her artistic insight while working on the cover artwork. Darnesha is a 2001 graduate of Western Michigan University, with a Bachelor of the Arts degree in Art.

To My Family

Leslie, my son, your beautiful heavenly experience will forever remain in my heart. God love you and bless you.

To my sons Ronnie and Robert, may God's hand guide you on the path of life that is before both of you.

To my daughters-in-law, Karen and Heather. You have given me encouragement and love.

To my grandchildren, Logan, Megan, Christopher, and Matthew, you are like the petals of a rose that is unfolding and grabs the dew on its leaves. May your lives be enriched as your spirits soar like a bird in flight. May you discover and know what life is all about.

To Tara, you were always with George in spirit, heart, and thoughts.

To Patrick and Stephen, Eileen's sons, may love and blessings be bountiful in your lives. George loved you very much, and thought of you as his own.

Table of Contents

Foreword

"If you would indeed behold the spirit of death, open your heart wide unto the body of life. For life and death are one, even as the river and the sea are one. In the depth of your hopes and desires lies your silent knowledge of the beyond; and like seeds dreaming beneath the snow, your heart dreams of spring. Trust the dreams, for in them is hidden the gate to eternity."

— Khalil Gibran
The Prophet (1923)

This story started as a journal. Matilda Ellis Balas said, "After my son George died, I had to write this book. I had to write of my spiritual encounters. I wanted everyone to know that there is a Heaven, and that those who pass on to that dimension are ready and able to communicate with us here on earth. When I was struggling with the thought of communicating my thoughts and feelings with others, I would go into a prayerful state, and was repeatedly told by God, 'Write the book.'"

Since she had never written a book before this happened, she prayed to God for support and guidance. The guidance and support came. One night, out of nowhere, her mind flooded with words. At four o'clock one morning she was awakened. Her thoughts and feelings began to pour out of her like water from a spigot; she wrote for hours. Her assumption is that she was somehow divinely inspired by the words and concepts that came relentlessly.

George was in Akron General Hospital, in Akron, Ohio, as a result of a serious head injury. As George lay dying, his brother Leslie was sleeping many miles away in his own bed in Euclid, Ohio. Leslie had what he can only describe as an out-of-body experience with his brother George. Leslie later revealed this experience to his mother. She was completely convinced that the "destiny of souls" goes back to its source. This out-of-body experience showed her that the "Rapture of Heaven" is always with us.

The existence of Heaven is something she is convinced of by the message that her son George gave her in a dream. She knew that he was reaching out to her. Before George's death, he knew of his mother's various health problems. One evening after his death, he came to her in a dream with words of encouragement. Later, his words would come back to her after she received the results of her tests from her physician.

Prayer helps us connect to a universal source. Much of what convinces her beyond a shadow of a doubt about these spiritual experiences and the content of her encounters comes from her prayer life. If you trust the process and allow the journey to take you where it will, it may bring you benefits beyond your expectations. If you combine this with the spiritual process, it can also bring you gratification and inner peace. A few moments of prayer or meditation — which serve the same purpose — help in the process of getting into spiritual writing, which in turn helps to get your message across. After George died, Matilda knew the story had to be told. This is what Matilda is doing by writing about her experiences.

Dreams influence everything, from our memories to our health and wellbeing in our relationships. They offer a window into our souls, and a doorway to the Other Side. We can make positive changes by paying attention to the messages contained in our dreams. We can reconnect with our departed loved ones through the most important portals we have to the Other Side.

Each of us is gifted, and has awakened with more knowledge than we had before we had fallen asleep. Many of us wake up with memories of time spent with loved ones we have lost.

It is interesting how reluctant we are to believe good news when it comes to us. When we discover that a deceased love one isn't deceased at all, and that they are very much about, loving and watching over us, we are determined to believe anything but the truth. If we accept that the spirit survives the death of the body, why do we not accept that those same spirits can interact with us? Spirits are powerful enough to overcome death, so why are they not powerful enough to come to us? Spirits transcend all of our negativity and our laws of limitation. This is to remind us how we find it so difficult to think outside of the earthly laws of physics and picture the spirit world, where none of these laws apply.

We know that while we dream, our subconscious minds are in charge, so it makes good sense that our dreamtime can be put to good use for the benefit of our overall health. Programming our dreams to accomplish healing while we sleep is probably one of the best ways to accomplish this healing through our subconscious discipline during sleep.

Grief over the loss of a loved one can be a volatile and shifting emotion. To suppress your need to mourn can ultimately be dangerous to your health. To act strong and indestructible on the outside while you are experiencing pain within can lead to disastrous consequences if not worked out. Like every other powerful emotion, the energy of grief has to go somewhere, and if it is not completely worked through and released from the body, you can count on it to take its toll, sooner or later, one way or another. So it is vital that we be patient with the process of grieving, both in ourselves and in all those around us.

Spirits have already accepted their deaths and transcended to the Other Side. When they visit us, it is from another dimension, which makes them more difficult to see and hear clearly. Watch and listen closely for spirits' efforts to communicate with you, without demanding that they be dramatic about it, or that every message they send involve major news. Let it be enough that they are with us and watching over us with eternal love. We know that the pathway to the soul is silence. It is of utmost importance that we maintain this silence because it drowns the inner instinctive natures of our beings, which hamper the messages that can come through to us. Silence and solitude are primary needs for the spiritual life, and are absolutely necessary to dispel the spiritual disorientation of our time. Therefore, it behooves us to maintain this silence and this solitude whenever possible.

Dreams connect all of us to one another because there is not a person on this earth who does not dream. They connect us to our ancestors because dreams are as old as humankind. They are one of the things that we have in common with people throughout the world, and with loved ones who have their own dreams to tell about if we will just take the time to listen.

Everything comes from God. The infinite is always available for us, and often through our prayers we make that important connection that we seek. So, in closing, let me offer up this prayer:

Father, we thank you for all the dreams that we have had, and for all the dreams that are yet to follow. We know that you give them to us for the growth and nourishment of our spirits. We are grateful for your perfect, unconditional, eternal love. In return, we offer our heartfelt gratitude for the many opportunities given to us to remain connected to our loved ones, and to know the peace that their presence brings during these gifted moments. My heartfelt thanks to you for this gift of love. Amen.

— The Reverend Frank Juhász Shepherd

Ecclesiastes 3:1-8 (KJV)

"To everything there is a season, and a time to every purpose
under the heaven:
a time to be born, and a time to die;
a time to plant, and a time to pluck up that which is planted;
a time to kill, and a time to heal;
a time to break down, and a time to build up;
a time to weep, and a time to laugh;
a time to mourn, and a time to dance;
a time to cast away stones, and a time to gather stones
together;
a time to embrace, and a time to refrain from embracing;
a time to get, and a time to lose;
a time to keep, and a time to cast away;
a time to rend, and a time to sew;
a time to keep silence, and a time to speak;
a time to love, and a time to hate;
a time of war, and a time of peace."

Nothing by Chance

When I read these verses from the Bible, I realized we are destined to follow patterns that have been set for us to live our lives and for our spirits to be fulfilled. I believe our destinies are programmed before we are born, and we are here to take this journey and learn as we go through life.

Our aspirations can be reached by the power of prayer. Our thoughts, our dreams and intuitions, and, most of all, God's inner voice guides us. If it is God's will to answer our prayers, you'll know when he does by the powerful force you feel exhilarating your body. Your spirits will be lifted and your prayers answered.

I felt compelled to write this book, not only for my family, but for others to share in my life experiences: the revelations that came to me, the intuition, the inner voice within me, my dreams that all became reality — and most of all, my son Leslie and the extraordinary after-death experience he had with his beloved brother, George, in a dimension beyond our lives here on earth.

All the happenings that have occurred in my lifetime so far show me that our spirits continue their journeys after our deaths on this earth, in another dimension of a glorious sphere of magnitude. If you believe in God, it is so, and this sphere is Heaven.

Chapter 1

The Journey of Life Begins

PRESENCE

My first spiritual encounter happened at the age of three. My mother had gone across the street and left me standing on the sidewalk by our house. Wanting to be with my mother, I darted into the street. As I ran in front of a parked car, I suddenly froze, unable to move as if someone held my hand. I looked up and heard my mother screaming, "A car is coming! Don't cross the street!" Immediately after the car passed, I ran to my mother and she said, "God saved you!" As she hugged me, I felt a strong presence, which, when I think about it, I can still feel to this day.

MY BEGINNINGS

My mother knelt on the sidewalk. She kissed and caressed me. Those three words she'd spoken, *"God saved you,"* were my first awareness of God. I have never forgotten them.

During the Great Depression in the 1930s, my family emigrated from Hungary. Upon our arrival on Ellis Island, Ellis became our new last name, because Illes was too hard to pronounce. My parents each brought the necessary essentials with them: a sixth-grade education, good morals and common sense. They taught me the love of God and the teachings of the Bible. Although we were poor, their kindness and values made us rich and were instilled into my life.

Life was lived with simplicity and appreciation for the things we had. Sunday was the best day of the week. After church services in the morning, we'd have a day of relaxation or going places together. I look back fondly at those years.

I remember my mother teaching me simple prayers and reading Bible stories about Jesus at bedtime. The awareness of God was very much a part of me, and consequently I was drawn to prayer like a magnet. When I was a little older, after I said my prayers I would talk to God about little things that concerned my child's mind. One day, I heard a voice answer me. Oh, I was so frightened that my mother had to calm me down, but then I realized what power prayer has, and that it was prayer that made the connection to God possible.

Other than my parents, I would not share my personal thoughts, not even with my childhood friends. I didn't think they would understand my thoughts or my life, and perhaps they'd laugh at me. I chose to remain silent. The silence remained throughout my adult life. Until now…

THE PIANO

At the age of five, I said, "WOW! Is this mine? Is this really mine?" I stood there, eyes open wide with total elation, looking at the piano.

Mom said, "Yes, it's yours. Dad and I bought it for you from friends who didn't want it anymore."

I sat down, touched the ivory keys, and then banged the keys to see what they sounded like. I loved it. Many times, I'd sit and listen to hear my brother John playing the piano. John was 13 years older than I. He'd play for hours on end, and he inspired the thoughts and emotions that prompted me towards a musical direction. At the age of eight, I was already singing on a Hungarian radio program, broadcasting from Akron, Ohio. I, too, would play and sing for hours at a time, and my mind would be filled with great expectations of the future.

My mother would take me to see Hungarian plays, and she'd clap for the performers. "Don't clap, Mama," I'd say to her. "Wait until I'm performing on stage, then clap for me."

KNOWING

At that young age of eight, I suddenly became aware of a strange feeling that came upon me at certain times and gave me the wisdom of knowing — but only at times when God wanted me to know. These feelings scared me, and I didn't know why they were happening. After telling my parents of my feelings, they said these insights came from God; they were pleased, and said I was blessed to have this knowledge.

STRONG INTUITION

During the summer of that same year, I attended Bible classes at our church. One day during class, I felt an extreme feeling of urgency to go home immediately. Where this feeling came from, I didn't know, but if I didn't go home, I felt I'd burst from this overwhelming anxiety that overtook my mind and body with the sense that something was wrong at home.

I waited until recess, and then I left the class and ran several blocks to get to our house. As I approached, I saw my father sitting on the porch swing. As I came closer, he appeared quite pale and he looked weak, as if from exhaustion.

Dad asked in a surprised tone of voice, "What are you doing home?"

"Dad, what's wrong with you? You look sick," I said. He told me he was having chest pains. I replied, "Dad, I had an awful feeling while I was in class, and I had to come home. I felt something was wrong."

My mother had gone shopping. She was unaware that Dad was not feeling well until she came home; she immediately went with him to the doctor's office. Luckily, everything turned out fine. Later, Dad felt better, and Mom and I felt relieved. This was my first encounter with the wisdom of knowing.

A CHILD'S CURIOSITY

One day that summer when I was eight, I was in my bedroom saying my prayers; outside at the same time, our house was being painted. My bedroom windows were open and I could hear the painters' voices.

As I said my prayers, out of curiosity I asked God, "How old will I be when my father dies?" I heard the answer *25*. I was surprised and shaken to hear this answer — to hear any answer. Where did this response come from?

I ran outside. The two painters were up on the ladders. I asked, "Just a few minutes ago, did anyone say the words *25*?" They wondered and questioned why I asked, and said no.

I never forgot about this happening. It haunted me through the years as time went by. When I was 25 years old, my father died. His death was not sudden: it was due to an injury he received at work from an inept co-worker. He never completely recovered, and the injury eventually led to his death by creating a blood clot on his brain. His death, which was revealed to me during prayer at the age of eight, had now actually happened.

As I pondered his death, the realization occurred to me that our existences were predestined. How else could I know of his death at the age of eight?

Chapter 2

The Teen Years

A HEAVENLY BEING

One day when I was a teenager, my dad and I were having a nice conversation. Dad told me what had happened to him growing up as a young teen in Hungary: he said that he was out in the fields and as he looked up towards the sky, he saw a beautiful lady dressed in a white robe floating towards the heavens.

It was a beautiful sight, and he watched in amazement as she rose into the heavens, until he could no longer see her.

My dad didn't know the meaning of this sighting, but he wanted me to know what he'd seen, and that's why he'd told me. Dad never forgot the beauty of the sighting, and his beliefs were justified: there are heavenly beings or spirits around us. I felt comfort in what he had said to me, and he said, "Don't ever forget what I just told you."

LET ALL MY LIFE BE MUSIC

As I went through my teen years, at times my mind was interested more in music than in spiritual happenings. I went to church on Sundays and I prayed to God every day, but nothing spiritual was happening in my life — no intuition, no dreams, nothing.

I concentrated on my music, and at 13 I was studying piano at the Cleveland Institute of Music. My ambition was to study voice. That was my love. I loved to sing, and I asked the advisors of the school if I could enroll. The information I received was that I had to be 16 years old to study voice.

Even if I tried out, I would not be accepted because of my age.

"Please?"

"Please?!"

After I auditioned, the vocal teachers listening to me remarked that my voice was exceptional. I was accepted. After being with the institute for two years, I wanted to expand into pop and semi-classical music; I then furthered my studies at the Theatrical Arts School for a while. Angelo Damales owned the art school; a fine teacher, he placed me for a job at the Theatrical Grill with one of his students, Michael. Michael was a wonderful singer. We would have to sing duets and also perform by ourselves, to the tune of $1500 a month — big, big bucks in the 1950s. The Theatrical Grill was popular, with well-known performers who had appeared there many times.

Michael came over to my house one afternoon and we rehearsed for many hours to perfect our performance. Every so often we would take a break, and then my dad would ask questions of Michael. "How long have you been studying music? What nationality are you, son?"

"Italian," replied Michael.

"Well, you have a beautiful voice," commented Dad.

Our day of music was winding down and Michael graciously said goodbye to all of us. Dad closed the door and said, "He's never coming back here again!"

"Why, Dad?" I questioned him.

Mom never said a word. "He's Italian and probably belongs to the Mafia, and I don't want him around you!" said Dad. The tone of his voice made this discussion final. When I watched the television show *All In The Family*, Archie Bunker reminded me of my father.

I became the soloist at our church and I started to sing at different events. Suddenly I became popular and received recognition. In high school, I earned a "Rating 1" at The Greater Cleveland Music Competition more than once. My accomplishments and performances were written about in the Hungarian newspaper, the *Szabadság*. At the events, the masters of ceremonies would announce, "At our banquet today, Matilda will entertain us with Gypsy music…"

"St. Stephens' drama group, April, 1952, presents Matilda Illes at the Moreland Theater…"

"We honor Governor Lausche, and on our program today is Matilda Illes…"

"Six members of the Cleveland Orchestra, Matilda Illes, soloist, and Frank Shepherd, a Juilliard graduate[*], to perform at Hungarian clubs…"

"*Cleveland Plain Dealer*, 1951: Public Hall's Little Theater presents *Broadway U.S.A.*, a Flynn production. Matilda Ellis' singing of "Mary Is A Grand Old Name" (in the picture hat and feather parasol of the Gibson era) won applause…"

And so it went, on and on, many performances within the community. But as good as my performances were, something within me was missing. Even though I always prayed, I felt hungry for more spiritual fulfillment. I was even considering becoming a nun to fill my personal need to quench this hunger. My parents would not hear of this,

---

[*] Shortly after his Juilliard graduation, Frank Shepherd studied for the ministry. To this day, he has been active in the churches of the Hungarian community.

saying, "You're not Catholic!" They just didn't understand me or my feelings.

A HOT SUMMER NIGHT

In the middle of the night, I was awakened by the sound of a violin playing romantic music and someone singing. My parents heard it, too, and ran into my bedroom to see what was going on.

"What the hell is going on in here?" asked Dad. We all looked out the bedroom window at the same time, practically falling over one another.

There were three guys serenading me. "Thanks, fellas, that's enough music. Do you know what time it is? Go home now," my father said.

"Well, now I have to put bars on the windows," he said to me, "to keep the guys out." And that's just how it was.

Life was wonderful. Being popular and loved made me feel like a movie star, although I thought my parents were overprotective of me.

NEW YORK

One weekend I went on a sightseeing trip to New York City with my best friend Genevieve. As we were wandering around Times Square, who should I see but my friend Frank Shepherd, the wonderful pianist I had performed with and known for a while. Frank mentioned that there was a Hungarian nightclub a couple of blocks past Times Square. Gen and I found it, so we walked in; a Gypsy band was playing fiery Hungarian *csárdás* music. My heart was beating fast as I was moved by the tempo; a feeling of elation filled my body. Beautiful music was filling the room as the Gypsies kept playing. I asked the owner of the club if I could sing, and he said yes. I was very well received by the audience. As the room filled with applause, the owner came over to me and gave me a job offer — singing a few hours a week for $75. I called home immediately. I was so excited and wanted to share the news with my parents, but the elation didn't last long — "Come home *now!*" Mom said.

THE COUNT FROM HAPSBURG

One of the most memorable times of my teen years was meeting Dr. Stephen Haller, a count from the House of Hapsburg. He was a doctor of law and a judge before coming to America.

Upon his arrival from Hungary, he settled in our Hungarian neighborhood on Buckeye Road and became a member of our church, the First Hungarian Reformed Church. My parents became acquainted with him, and soon they became best friends. Mom would cook the traditional elaborate Hungarian meal of chicken soup, roasted chicken, and stuffed cabbage with delicious pastry for dessert, and Dr. Haller would be there to enjoy it.

Every time he came for dinner, I was bursting with pride that we were entertaining a count at our home. Dr. Haller had a refined manner. He was always humble and gracious, and it was an honor to have him as a friend.

On occasion, we would visit Dr. Haller. One day, my mother and I stopped to visit with him at his apartment: it was small, modest, and sparsely furnished. It was hard to imagine what he'd once possessed and what he had now.

As we sat talking, I told him I was going to take part in a church play about Hungary. He said he had clothes and jewels that I could wear.

Across from where we were sitting I saw a huge trunk. "Open it," said Dr. Haller. I quickly did so, and my eyes fell on the glory of his past years, which had now come down to the contents of that trunk.

The trunk was filled with velvet robes, trimmed in what I thought was cheetah fur. There were large rubies and emeralds on a pure gold band to be worn during ceremonial occasions. The band draped from the wearer's back, down his shoulder, across his chest, and around his waist. Other jewels and precious possessions were in the trunk. He was very gracious and said, "Take whatever you need for your performance." I did, and wore his jewels proudly for the play.

During this time, there was an assistant minister at our church, Reverend Ferenc Vitéz, also from Hungary. Reverend directed the Hungarian choir, and I played the piano for their weekly rehearsals. Reverend would always walk me home after rehearsals, and he came to our home every now and then for a visit; he and I also dated a couple of times. I always called him "Reverend." It never occurred to me that he was planning our future.

One Sunday, Dr. Haller came for dinner and, much to my surprise, asked my parents for my hand in marriage to Reverend Vitéz. Of course, my parents would have been delighted for this to occur, but I was shocked at what was taking place. I believed arranged marriages were a thing of the past, not the 1950s. I was still in high school and Reverend was about 31 years old.

Shortly afterward, Reverend was leaving for a new position at a church in New Jersey. The night he was departing, he called from the train station at the Cleveland Terminal and asked if he could come over to talk to me. I replied that it was a school night and I had homework to do. I wished him well on his new position and venture.

Across the room, my mother was shaking her fist at me, angry that I had just brushed Reverend Vitéz off. "You just threw your future away!" she yelled at me.

"Ma! I'm still in school. He's too old for me! And what about love?" I felt that I would be engulfed by a sea of love, but that was not happening.

Chapter 3

Our Early Years

THE MEETING

"I don't want to go! I don't want to go!" I shouted at my father. "I'm not going to the church banquet." Tears were streaming down my face. I was a young woman twenty years of age, and I knew what I wanted to do. My father was adamant about me going with the family to the church banquet.

So after all of that, there I was, sitting in my chair at the table in the church's banquet hall with my parents. A young man came by and asked, "Is this chair taken?"

There was no room for him where his parents were sitting. I replied, "The chair is not taken," and he sat down.

The servers started to bring the food, and I glanced at him; he said his name was Ron and I introduced myself as Millie, and suddenly I knew he would be my husband. We were formally introduced after the banquet by a relative.

After dating for three weeks, we became engaged. I had suddenly found that sea of love and felt engulfed by it. On October 9th in the fall of 1954, we pledged our love to each other. The church was filled to capacity with friends and admirers. Seven hundred people came to the reception, many without invitation, but no one was turned away. Everyone was fed and later danced to the wonderful Gypsy music.

In the Hungarian community, my parents owned a two-family home. They insisted that we move upstairs from them. Within a year's time, our own family was started.

****
****

Through the years, every now and then I would think of the strange feelings and intuitions I experienced as a child. It had been several years since anything had presented itself to me, and I doubted anything would ever happen again, until...

****
****

THE HEALING DREAM

In September of 1955, our first son, Ronnie Jr., was born. One day when he was fourteen months old, his father, unaware of the door's archway, playfully tossed him into the air. Ronnie hit his head, cried, and then seemed to be fine. It wasn't until a few months later that Ronnie started to have convulsions.

We took him to Cleveland Clinic. On examination, the doctor said, "Due to the injury that occurred, there is a slight split in the skull which, in time, will heal." As for the convulsions, the doctor was uncertain. He said Ronnie could have epilepsy for the rest of his life, and prescribed Dilantin.

A few months later, our son contracted measles and had a high fever. We took him to Dr. Deme, who gave him penicillin; unfortunately, Ronnie had an allergic reaction, and was very ill not only from the high fever, but also from the penicillin.

Both my husband and I were exhausted. My brother-in-law Bob came to help us out.

One night while Bob was there, I laid across our bed, exhausted. I fell asleep and dreamt that I was praying in the garden of Gethsemane, and a voice said to me, "Everything will be all right."

As I was dreaming this, I heard Bob calling me. "Millie, Millie — come quickly! Ronnie is having a convulsion!" I ran into Ronnie's room; he was frothing at the mouth and had turned gray in color, even a slight shade of purple. Ron yelled, "Get a spoon, he's swallowed his tongue!" I was shaking as I handed him the spoon and he pried Ronnie's tongue out so that he could breathe.

I was angry and trembling when I ran out to the back porch and cried out to God, "Why?" The sky was full of stars and I said to God firmly, "You just told me in my dream that everything was going to be all right, and we almost lost our son!" As I stood there looking at the sky and the countless stars, I felt in my heart that this dream was an acknowledgement of God's healing power.

We drove to St. Luke's Hospital, a couple of blocks away. Ronnie's temperature was over 102•. The doctors packed him in ice for several hours to bring down his fever. At that time, my mother was involved with Kathryn Kuhlman's prayer ministries, and she contacted the group for a healing prayer for Ronnie.

The following day, Ronnie came home from the hospital. A member of the prayer group contacted me by phone and said, "Your son will be healed, and he'll never have another convulsion."

It has been almost fifty years. Our son is alive and well. The dream was real and the prayers were answered. Ronnie never had another convulsion. After this miracle, how can one doubt the healing power of God?

At the time of this healing, my heart burst with joy to have been given a revelation in my dream, and then for our son Ronnie to have been healed with God's miraculous healing power. Although my husband said that he believed, I felt skeptical that his spiritual beliefs were not fully developed, and that he put more credence in himself and worldly things that surrounded his life rather than faith.

Spiritually, we were not on the same level. Ron had too many distractions in his life, and his knowledge of spirit had not yet come full circle. It would take life's journey, with its lessons, to develop and know the spirit within himself.

OUR YOUNG FAMILY

In time we were blessed with three other healthy, beautiful sons: George, Leslie, and Robert. My parents now became Grandma and Grandpa Ellis. The children were spoiled with love.

One day, two cars — a jeep and another child's car with pedals — were delivered to our house for Ronnie and George. Within days, the tires had come off; in fact, everything that would come off did — including the steering wheels. After all, these boys were mechanics. They had problems rebuilding the cars, so their dad and Grandpa Ellis would have to do it; they put them back together again.

After Leslie was born, the space in our small apartment was not enough. We purchased a rundown house in Cleveland Heights. The house was very large, unlike any house we ever lived in before. Ron and I played games trying to find each other. "Where are you?" we would call out to each other. Five years later, Robert was born, and we had ample room for all of us.

How proud we were as parents. Many times, Ron would give them horsy rides. "My turn, Dad. Give me a ride," they each said as they eagerly awaited their turns. "I'm next!"

Leslie, as little as he was, would be laughing and giggling with Ronnie and George as they romped through the living room. Ronnie and George were two years apart in age and did everything together. One day they had so much fun laughing and jumping on our bed, they got completely carried away. Despite warning them to stop, I was ignored. I heard a loud crash. I ran upstairs to find that the frame of the bed had broken. The mattress and box spring were on the floor.

"Oh my gosh — oh my God! Boys, you broke our bed." They didn't realize the complexity of my problem; they continued laughing and jumping while I talked. "I can't fix this. What am I going to do? Your father is going to kill me when he sees the bed is broken."

Just then, I heard a truck coming down the street: it was the milkman. His cousins lived a house away from Grandma Ellis, so we kind of knew each other. I ran downstairs to meet him at the door. I felt anxious and tense.

I smiled and gritted my teeth as I blurted out, "Will you please come up to my bedroom?" He had a startled look on his face. "No, no — it's not what you think. My boys were jumping on the bed, and the frame of my bed broke. I need help. I can't fix this problem, and I need you to fix it for me."

I ran down to the basement for a hammer and nails. I watched him bang the nails into the frame, and as he did, I knew his thoughts: *She sure has a lot of nerve to ask me to fix this while my customers are waiting for me to deliver their milk.*

I was thinking: *I sure hope he can fix this bed in a few minutes and get out of here; I wouldn't want Ron to come home and find the milkman in our bedroom.*

Sundays we would all go to church. Ron participated in everything we did. He also was a Sunday school teacher. Our sons would go every Sunday.

The holidays were always special. One particular Christmas comes to my mind. We would have a tree that was brightly lit, and each of us would carefully hang every ornament in the exact spot it should be placed on the tree. Leslie created a paper chain of red and green links that would adorn the fireplace mantel. Little people made of yarn would be placed under the tree. Ron made a fire in the fireplace that blazed and the embers glowed with warmth.

A knock was heard at our kitchen door. Ronnie, George and Les would run to see who it was. Robert was just a tiny tot, and he had a big smile on his face. The boys opened the door. It was Santa, his red sack over his shoulder. Everyone noticed that Santa was not wearing his boots, but brown shoes. Santa greeted everyone with a hearty "Merry Christmas." The boys knew it was Grandpa Balas. Grandma Balas was right behind him, bringing all kinds of goodies to munch on.

Our children's eyes were bright and their laughter filled the room as the contents of Santa's sack were revealed. First, out came a drum with sticks that would beat; a golden horn was revealed, with songs of its own; a cannon with a ramrod and several cannon balls — the balls would shoot out and bring excitement and joy to all. Now the fun began as the boys marched through the house, beating the drum, blowing the horn, and singing. Every now and then, the cannon would go off.

The grown-ups sat by the fireplace watching the children play with an endless spirit of happiness. Everyone was munching on goodies and drinking hot chocolate while Christmas music filled the room. This was a wonderful Christmas indeed. It would be a memory that would stay with us for many a year in our hearts and minds.

But as time went on, I began to realize that my marriage felt like a fantasy. We appeared to be a wholesome family to everyone else, but something was not right. The man, my husband, whom I loved so much and who loved me had a problem with alcohol, which affected all of our lives.

As young children, Ronnie and George had been taking Judo lessons. One evening, Ron drove them to their classes. He dropped them off and went for a drink at a bar with his friends. At home, I was thinking, *Where could they be? They should have come home a while ago.*

Finally I heard Ron's car pull up in the drive. I ran to the door and asked, "Where are the boys?"

"What boys?" asked Ron. He was tipsy.

"Ronnie and George," I yelled.

"Oh my God," he said as he ran to his car. "I forgot to bring them home!"

THE STAR

It has been a few years since I had performed, but now I was invited to be with the best of the best, the *crème de la crème*, to perform for a sold-out event at the Cleveland Hotel Ballroom. This event was October 1966's "Night in Budapest." Appearing on the program would be Mary Ann Mobile and Paul Lucas, the Hungarian stars from Hollywood, and MGM producer Joseph Pasternak. Everybody who was somebody in the community came to this fabulous night. I couldn't wait to entertain everyone and to sing with this large Gypsy orchestra, which consisted of Joe Rabb and Ernie King's musicians and Gypsies.

Then it was my turn to perform. I was surrounded with admiration and smiling glances from people surrounding me. The music started and my heart filled with song. The sound of my voice went out into the audience, singing the haunting Gypsy music everyone could feel in their souls. Then came the applause: the gratification of a job well done and the thunderous applause for a wonderful performance. I was so pleased with myself. I accepted compliments graciously on my way back to our table. "You were wonderful!" I heard said. "Great job!" someone else remarked.

My husband was having a marvelous time: he was filled with spirits straight out of the bottle. Laughing and joking, he was drunk. "Ha, ha, ah, ha, ha!" He was about to sit down, but he'd missed his chair and ended on the floor. "Ah, ha, ha, ha, ah, ha," as he was being helped back to his chair. "I fell off the chair," he said with uncontrollable laughter. "Ah, ha, ha, ha, ha, ha."

On the night of all nights what an unfortunate circumstance lay before my eyes! "Lord, get me out of this place. I've had enough."

I was simply embarrassed to tears; I had to leave immediately with friends. The night had lost its glamour as reality now prevailed.

Within days, I received a letter from MGM Studios and none other than Joseph Pasternak, complimenting me on my performance, and thanking me for being part of a wonderful night. I thought how thoughtful of him to send me this letter. He lifted my spirits and made me feel extremely important — and for the moment, a star.

Being busy with my family left little time or consideration for me to continue my musical ambitions. I realized Ron didn't know the extent of my musical abilities, the applause I received, the work, and the practice that went into each performance. At times in the past, I sang for a large audience — 2000-plus. The gratitude of people around me was all a wonderful experience.

Ron's parents had moved away from the Hungarian community when Ron was a young boy, therefore, growing up he was not exposed to the Hungarian culture as much as I was.

As time passed through the years, my musical abilities were slipping away and eventually faded into the background as life took over.

THE PARTY

Although I have already written of my father's death, the following happened a few months prior to his passing:

My husband and I were going to a party across town on the west side. We left our two young sons with the babysitter, and gave her the telephone number in case of an emergency.

When we arrived, I was relaxed and enjoying the party, but soon I felt discontented and uneasy, and had a feeling of just wanting to go home. My husband did not take my feelings seriously and said, "We'll leave later."

A little while later, I was getting upset and said, "We have to leave now. Something is terribly wrong at home!" He said the babysitter has the phone number and she had not called. Disregarding him, I went to our car. Soon he reluctantly followed, and we drove home.

Upon arrival my mother met us at the door and said, "I could barely wait until you came home; the babysitter lost the phone number where you would be. Your father took ill and was rushed to the hospital."

****
****

The power of prayer was living proof that it does work. If it's God's will, he will answer your prayer, and you will know by the powerful force you feel exhilarating your body, just as I did.

****
****

We purchased our home in the sixties; it was neglected and in need of repair. In those early years of marriage, it took a lot of money to raise four sons, to meet the necessities of life and to have money not only for repairs but other unforeseen events.

We had our debts, the bills mounted, creditors started calling; soon almost every day someone was calling to receive payment. In those days, calls were demanding and nasty.

Being a housewife and at home everyday, I started to pray to God for relief from the harassing calls. "Render it, God, that the creditors will not be able to hurt us. Please do not let them garnish my husband's wages, or put a lien on our home. Please, God." I said this over and over every day. "Render them helpless."

At that time, we owed a finance company a few hundred dollars plus late charges that had accrued. They repeatedly kept calling for payment.

One day the collector called. I made arrangements to pay on the loan by a specific day of that month. I guess he was not satisfied, and he called again the following day. He only said a few words, and again I told him I'd send the payment owed for that month.

The following day, I left to do errands; as I was walking down the driveway, a big black car pulled up in front of our home.

"Mrs. Balas?" the driver asked. It was the collector from the finance company.

I was shaking and so upset to see him coming to our house. I said, "We made payment arrangements over the phone."

"That's not what I came to talk to you about," he answered.

"Then what?" I asked.

"I wanted to see what you looked like. Yesterday before I called you, I wrote down several demands I expected from you in order to pay back the loan. When you answered the phone, I could not utter a word of my demands. As hard as I tried, nothing would come out of my mouth."

As I looked directly into his eyes, I was stunned to hear what this man was saying to me. I would not have known the powerful impact of my prayers if this collector would not have come to our house to tell me. I told him it was the power of prayer. "It has been hard for us to pay back this loan, but you will be paid." I said goodbye, and as I continued walking, I thanked God for the powerful answer to my prayers. Almost in disbelief of what just happened, my body filled with joy. I felt an extreme high, a glorious uplifting feeling as I continued walking. I felt empowered by God.

As it turned out, within two weeks the collector called back and said he had written off the loan. The books were closed. He took me quite by surprise. I never expected anything of this sort to happen. I thanked him from the bottom of my heart.

Prayer is powerful! God will meet our needs through prayer if it is his will to answer us.

THE DREAM OF ALICE

Alice was a neighbor of mine, and through the years we became good friends. I had a dream that Alice was walking down the front walk of her house towards me, dressed in black and crying.

I asked her, "What's wrong, Alice?"

She replied, "My mother died."

At the time I had this dream I told Alice. She said, "I hope it doesn't come true." But so it was: two weeks later, Alice came down the front walk of her home towards me to tell me her mother had just died.

Chapter 4

Uncertain Years

My dad asked, "What are you doing?" as I pushed the dining room table up into my parents' attic.

"I'm moving back home — I'm getting a divorce. Ron has a girlfriend, and I'm leaving him," I replied.

Then I woke up. I did not like my dream, or the appearance of the blond woman that had appeared in my dream.

Our family unit was falling apart as the months of the 1970s unfolded. My husband shared very little of his time with any of us, and said his work kept him busy. At times I felt like we were married only in name. The expectations for my marriage were not met. It seemed as if a force was pulling us apart, like an unstoppable rollercoaster headed for destruction.

My heart filled with sadness as my marriage continued to deteriorate because of the circumstances of life that surrounded me. Then, one September morning before Ron went to work, he told me he wanted to live on his own and was thinking of moving out. I could not change his mind. I felt like everything around me had fallen apart, and that life had drained me. I needed to get away from it all.

I told our sons that we were going to California to visit Uncle John, and to gather their clothes. Meanwhile, my mother would often take the bus to come visit us, always carrying bags of goodies and bringing lunch for us. Today as she was walking up our driveway, I happened to glance out the window.

I was panic-stricken. I just wanted to leave, and when Mom came into the house and found out what was happening, she pleaded for us not to leave, but I wouldn't listen to her.

I made Mom promise not to tell anyone where we were going. I felt bad that I had hurt her feelings. By noon I boarded a plane with my sons, and flew to California to spend time with my brother. Ironically, Ron came back home, but by then we were gone.

John lived in Huntington Beach, and I needed a retreat, somewhere I could be in peaceful surroundings without any problems.

I needed a place where I could find comfort, be secure, and be able to gather my thoughts. To my dismay, my seemingly peaceful existence was shattered by my own brother. Damn him! Damn him! He crossed a boundary. Our sibling relationship was over forever. I despised him. I found solace through prayer, and this chapter of my life was closed. And so life went on.

Lack of money had become a problem, so it was difficult for all of us to return together. In October, I put Ronnie and George on the train; I had to wait until November to leave with Leslie and Robert. Finally we were all at home and together again.

On my arrival, I filed for divorce; my husband and I had our arguments and disagreements, plus there was the third party from my dream: the blonde woman was on the scene. The sentimental nostalgic feelings of the holiday season gave me a false sense of hope, though, and a little bit of stability — so I thought — to our marriage, and I dropped the divorce proceedings.

Through the years, our marriage had warm happy times, and we also shared our bad times. My husband had a miraculous recovery from his beer drinking days. I felt he had now lost his path in life and didn't know which direction to chose.

The Christmas season had come and gone. I wanted to live a less complicated family life, with more togetherness and more stability, and to find joy in everything life offered us. I wanted to live life as a family should.

As the new year began, I knew my marriage was coming to an end. Ron decided to move out, to go his own way and gave me the old cliché, "I have to find myself."

We lived apart for several months, although he'd stay a few days with us every now and then. Another reality was to unfold. Ron had become an accomplished black belt in karate, and by this time had his own classes in a school. He asked me to go see one of his tournaments. Upon my arrival, the gym was very crowded, and Ron had to be with his students. As I glanced across the room, I then saw the other woman keeping very close company with my husband. I felt totally neglected, unwanted, and in an embarrassing situation watching them, and thought, *Why did I even bother to come?*

I saw her leaving; I ran after her. As she was going down the steps, I followed quickly and yelled at her, "You whore, you bitch — what are you doing with my husband? You're nothing but a whore!" As I said this, she ran out the door. Several people were around, and it felt good to have a chance to get back at him and to embarrass her.

****
****

In 1975, my brother resurfaced in my life once again. Since our sibling relationship had ceased in 1970, I had no use for him, and only spoke to him in concern for our mother.

By now he had remarried, and came to Cleveland with his wife. He demanded to inherit everything of mother's because he was the son and the oldest sibling. John's decision gave great distress to our mother. This meant I would receive nothing, nor would her beloved grandchildren after her death.

****
****

I went to bed one night and as I closed my eyes, a vision appeared to me. A heavenly being was standing on a cloud, a long white beard covering his chest, and dressed in a white robe against a blue sky. His arm outstretched, his index finger pointed at me.

I quickly opened my eyes and closed them again, and the vision reappeared. I was shaken; not a word was said, only the pointing of his finger at me. My heart felt that this was a vision of God. But was it God?

I jumped out of bed and ran downstairs to tell my family. "What could this vision mean?" I asked.

Ron replied, "God's telling you that you're going to win the lottery." Our children laughed. I knew there was a deeper meaning, but it would be a few months before I'd know what that meaning was.

My brother John arrived with his wife, Kathy, and moved into Mother's house. John had married his first cousin. Mother was glad to have them living with her, although she did not approve of their marriage. Soon the harassment over my mother's money would begin. John had sold his home in California and now had plenty of money of his own.

Kathy had grown up in Hungary under communist rule, and said to me, "What is yours is mine."

I said, "Everyone works for what they have. It is theirs, not yours."

The harassment over Mother's money would begin early in the morning. My brother spoke bitter words to her, making his demands. Every day, Mother called me about the verbal abuse and said that she could barely tolerate the situation. Kathy and John were so money-hungry that they went to see the minister at the church to see if they could receive her social security check. My mother's mind was sound and she was able to conduct her own financial matters, so John and Kathy's request was rejected by the minister.

The next day, John came to our home. He was concerned about his inheritance. I was alone in the house; the boys were out and about. Ron was at work. John and I were in the kitchen.

As we were talking, he picked up a kitchen chair and banged it on the floor, over and over again, at the same time loudly demanding money. "I am the son, I am the oldest, and mother's inheritance belongs to me."

I suddenly realized that I was trapped in a corner of the room and would not be able to walk away from him. I was afraid — afraid he would hurt me. I could feel fear taking ahold of my body. For a split second, the thought of God flashed through my mind. I heard a car drive into our driveway. John heard it, too. It broke the tension he had created, and he put the chair down.

Unexpectedly, it was Ron; this was not in his daily routine to come home from work. I was relieved to see him. John greeted him as if nothing had occurred, and quickly left our house, never to return. God was watching over me that day. In doing so, he sent Ron home to keep me from harm.

As time went by, every now and then I'd think of the vision, and as the discord between my mother and brother grew worse, I now understood my job to become the peacemaker. I wanted my mother and brother to be amicable with each other. In a few weeks, the situation between them became so tense that I had to tell John and Kathy to move out of my mother's home.

Mother was so angry with John because he treated her with meanness that she decided to change her will. John was to receive $500, the return of a loan he'd given to his parents when they purchased their home, and also a few hundred dollars for all the gifts he'd sent her through the years, including Mother's Day flowers. I tried to talk Mother out of this decision, but she insisted. "This is the way it has to be," she said.

Unfortunately, a few months after John and Kathy moved out, Mother had a stroke and died. John and Kathy did not attend the funeral. I tried to bring peace between my mother and brother, but peace never happened between them. I had to cope with my mother's death and the settlement of her will, which was very bitter between my brother and me. No matter how bitter the arguments, however, I felt I was chosen for this task. Eventually everything was settled according to my mother's will, despite the greed of my brother and Kathy.

The year 1975 was ending, and I never saw my brother again. I later heard he went back to Hungary with Kathy for his retirement.

A DEATH REVEALED

Springtime, 1976: when flowers and trees burst out in bloom and nature is reborn; it was the week before Easter. Suddenly, my mother was stricken by a stroke and was rushed to the hospital. After a couple of days, Mom felt a little bit better, and I anticipated her return home shortly.

While Mom was recovering, I dreamt of being at my mother's funeral, and the gathering of several family friends. A neighbor, Barbara, asked me, "When did your mother die?"

I replied, "Good Friday."

I awoke from this dream and knew immediately that I had to notify my son Ronnie to have him come home. He was in the Army, stationed at Fort Ord, California. My husband was upset when he found out that Ronnie was flying home; he told me it was ridiculous to have Ronnie fly 3,000 miles — it was only a dream and it was not going to happen. I felt in my heart that Ron didn't know what I knew. In my heart, I knew it would happen. The dream was real. Within two days, Ronnie arrived home. By this time, Mom had slipped into a coma and it was Good Friday. Her death occurred in the early hours of Easter morning in 1976.

At my mother's funeral was a gathering of several family friends; one in particular, our neighbor Barbara, who had asked "When did your mother die?" in my dream, then asked the same question at my mother's funeral.

The day of the funeral, as we walked out of the church I never expected to hear what our son George told me — that he saw Grandma sitting in the choir loft, smiling and looking down upon us. What George said left me speechless for a moment, and I questioned him over and over, only to get the same answer.

I was truly amazed by his experience with my mother's spirit. At the time of her death, George had sobbed uncontrollable tears at the hospital; now her spirit had come back to comfort him and to let him see that she was happy and well. George was the only one in the family who had this vision at the funeral, and as he grew older she would still be with him in his dreams.

THE DIVORCE

A short time after my mother passed, Ron wanted to live on his own and moved out again. There were times that we had no communication with each other nor did I know where he was; there were times when he lived with us and we were a family again.

We spent many weekends in the country on my parents' property in Portage County, which now belonged to me. The property was 5 ¼ acres of mostly woods, and was surrounded by other beautiful woods and farmland. So many happy days occurred there: the gathering of our family, with the grandparents joining us; our sons walked through the woods and chopped wood for the fire, played horseshoes, caught frogs, and had frog legs for lunch. There was always the delicious aroma of food cooking on the wood-burning grill my dad had built. My brother-in-law and his wife Norma joined in the fun. There was laughter and love and a sense of being whole. We felt the sense of belonging and knowing that all was good. Everyone loved these times and never wanted them to end.

The decade of the '70s was coming to a close. I reflected back on the last ten years, and felt I'd had enough! I wanted to live life. I didn't want to be surrounded by the loneliness of not having a husband at home with me, the indecision and living life at my husband's convenience. I felt he was caught up in a whirlwind of his own doings and that he was running with the wind. Regardless that he thought — or may have thought — that he wanted to come home and we should stay together, there would always be something to keep us apart. I could not stop him from doing his thing, nor could I stop myself from making my decision. The dream that I had in 1970 took almost ten years of my life to unfold. Although I tried, I could not stop the events that made the dream become reality.

REFLECTIONS ON THE SEVENTIES

My life in the 70s was difficult. I was not concerned if I was rich or poor materially. I was more concerned with having the richness of my spirit and the goodness that poured out from within me to reach others. I cannot explain the childlike feeling that had stayed with me throughout my life just by praying and talking to God every day.

Even though we go through stressful and hurtful events in our lives, we can cry and carry on with our emotions. But if we are tuned into God, we know that, in the end, some good shall return to us from the good we've put forth unto others in our lifetime.

As our sons were growing up, I taught them to love and help each other, for the fruits of goodness that we sow will bring the harvest of happiness. When our children were young we would go to our place in the country; they would each grab an axe and try to chop down small trees for firewood.

Grandma Balas would say, "Chop only what's needed. You're hurting the tree when you chop it, and it will cry."

"Why?" they would ask.

Grandma would say, "A tree is a living thing; it is alive and can feel." They learned respect for all living things and appreciated life. By the time our sons became teenagers, the beauty of their youths was unfolding like the petals of a flower.

Of course they all wanted to have a car by the time they each turned sixteen, but nothing would be handed to them on a silver platter. I'd say to them, "Boys, you have to find a job and save your money for the things you want in life." They all found jobs; they were eager to work and to save their money.

Ronnie and George had a paper route. Many times, early in the morning after delivering papers they would stop at a bakery and tap on the window. The baker would bring them fresh donuts straight from the oven. Leslie worked at an ice cream store for one dollar an hour and thought he was rich. Robert was too young to work, but he would start supper every day before I came home from work. Everyone was busy going to school and working. Our sons had a strong brotherly bond with each other.

But now my marriage was changing. The morals and lifestyles of our country were changing: the decadence of drugs crept slowly into our neighborhood and into our lives. Marijuana was prevalent everywhere, even in the schools.

Ronnie and George's friends often came to our home. Our finished attic was like a recreation room, and the boys would go up there to listen to their favorite music.

One day, I went upstairs to see how everyone was doing. As I opened the door I heard the sounds of music. A sweet aroma hit my nose. I heard footsteps scrambling and someone saying, "Uh-oh." I caught them smoking marijuana.

Before I knew what was happening, marijuana was growing in my yard. A big plant was growing by my driveway, out in the open for everyone to see, but no one ever questioned what kind of plant it was. I thought it was a big weed and pulled it out. Then I found a marijuana plant growing in the house. Actually, it was on the roof of our house; one day when I looked out the window, there it was. But by then I knew what kind of plant it was. I questioned Leslie, "What is this plant growing in this pot?"

"It's a potato plant, Mom."

"Oh, yeah. Get rid of this marijuana plant right now, Les." Boy, he sure was surprised his mother actually knew what marijuana looked like.

Through the years the boys would think about their teens and reminisce. One day, Ronnie said, "Ma, how did you survive our years of growing up? Remember all the headaches we gave you, and what you had to go through with us?"

"How could I forget, Ronnie?"

"Mom, do you remember one night when I came home, and I was so sick you thought I had food poisoning, but found out I was drinking? Then you said, 'Well, then die!' You slammed the door as you walked out of my room and left me there to suffer.

"What about Robert when he partied hard one night? His friends drove him home and left him sleeping on the front lawn. You heard the commotion, jumped out of bed, and ran outside. You grabbed Robert by his shirt collar, dragged him all the way upstairs to his room, threw him on his bed, and said 'I'll deal with you in the morning.'

"Ma, remember when you kept smelling whiffs of smoke? You thought a neighbor was barbecuing, but Les was experimenting in the attic with cigarettes that day. He thought he had put the cigarette out before he threw it through the window. It was not out, and it fell between the dry wall and the windowsill, where it smoldered for several hours. When the firemen came, they dragged the fire hose through the living room over the new carpeting and up into the attic. At the same time, the black smoke from the attic came down and settled all over our new furniture. When it was over, Les was shaking like a leaf. He was so scared. The fireman towered over him with his height and his muscular body, and reprimanded him for smoking."

"Well, Ronnie, it's nice to reminisce, but when these problems happened they were not laughing matters. It's one thing to talk about them years later; it's another thing to live through the experience."

I had quite a few sleepless nights until they grew out of their teen years. I encouraged them to always talk to me and to make good choices in life. I hoped the teachings they had as children in Sunday school and church would stay with them. In time it did.

Ronnie and George both served in the Army. Unfortunately, George became addicted to alcohol and drugs; he tried for many years to give up his addictions, but could not, and his decisions affected all of us.

VIBRATIONS OF CHANGES

The divorce was by now final. I'd always rolled with life's punches, but now, 24 years of marriage — which I thought was sacred and lasted forever — tumbled down around me, and my marriage ceased to exist. I felt anger and bitterness for nearly five years.

Although my spirit of life was shattered, my spirit believing in God was still strong. It was wonderful knowing about things in my life before they occurred, but at that time I asked God not to have any more revelations in my dreams or insights about what would happen in my life. I simply didn't want to know.

I had devoted all of my energy to our sons' lives and to my job at a computer company. Fortunately, my boss Skai became a pillar of strength for me. There were mornings I went to work and cried buckets of tears. I felt so distraught, so drained by my family problems, and I had no one to talk to. Skai took me under her wing, took the time to listen to me, gave me words of encouragement to strengthen me, and gave me wisdom.

Skai was herself a strong woman, who, in past years, had coped with her own divorce, and had her struggles in life raising a family. Now she was an angel to strengthen me during the hardest time of my life, and to make me believe in myself. "You can do it, whatever lies ahead. Be strong!"

were her words to me. With her words and prayers, I was able to draw strength to cope with life's problems.

There was a period of time I worked seven days a week. I needed money to survive. Life was hectic for a while. I felt like I was running a boarding house, as our sons kept coming and going. They had outgrown their teenage years; by now, they were decent young men ready to accept life's challenges. Eventually they all found their paths, and one by one left home.

Ronnie had met Karen. They married and lived with me for a while, then moved to Vermont. Robert finally grew up and joined the Air Force in 1984. He was stationed at Edwards Air Force Base. Only Leslie and George remained in Cleveland at this time.

The first Christmas after our divorce, my mother-in-law called and invited me for dinner. "I don't want you to be alone during Christmas. Please come. The boys will be here, also — their father already invited them." I accepted the invitation even though in the past we'd had words and did not see eye to eye on things. I had not been at my in-laws' home for several months.

In past years, many Christmases were spent at Grandma Balas' house. As we sat down at the dining room table, the aroma of the holiday turkey and wonderful food was waiting for us. This reminded me of past years, full of fun and laughter. Now I was sitting here divorced, and to remember the past years made me feel sad, even out of place. I was at a loss for what to say. I went home and cried that I had even considered going there in the first place. Being there became a painful experience for me. Once again, in my mind I relived the wonderful memories of Christmases past, but this Christmas was just the beginning of Christmases to come.

Every day I was busy, if not working at my job, then working at home. One day, a young man came to my front door and rang the doorbell. He was standing on my porch trying to sell me magazines, which I didn't need and did not buy. We chatted for a few minutes, and when he was leaving he turned and said, "You are pretty."

I closed the door, ran upstairs, and stood staring at myself in the mirror. I'd never thought of myself. It was always others whose needs came before mine. But now, as I stood there looking at myself, I realized my lifestyle would be changing. I was now a single woman. I had a free life, and wasn't it wonderful God gave me free will to determine which direction to take? And, yes — I was pretty!

****
****

God, help me with my life. Surround me with your blessings. Lead me; guide me to where I should be at this time in my life. Thus, a new chapter in my life was to begin.

****
****

Chapter 5

Starting Over

THE SINGLE LIFE

Where do I start? Where do I go to meet single people? All my friends were married, and in time our friendships would cease because our lifestyles would be so different.

One Sunday morning, I read in the newspaper that the St. Clare church singles group was looking for new members. I had no car and no way to get there. When I called about the meeting, a woman said transportation would be provided. The day of the meeting, Ed came to pick me up: he was my driver, and he drove me to the meeting.

Several people belonged to this group, and many tears were shed during the session as people grieved over their divorces, looking for answers to life. I had grieved for so many months over my marriage, trying to make decisions. Should I or should I not divorce? At this time, I could no longer grieve. After attending two more sessions, I said, "I can't grieve anymore." I didn't want to be depressed or feel sad anymore. I'd had enough! I wanted to feel good; I wanted laughter in my life and to have enjoyment, the way life should be lived. I wanted to have fun!

From then on, I attended the regular meetings of the social group. After the meetings, people would go dance at the Shaker House. In a short time, Ed was not only my driver — he had become my best friend. We would stop to dance after each social meeting. It had been several years since I had last danced, and now the music had changed. No more sounds of the big band music; now it was rock-and-roll.

The first time I danced, I felt like all eyes were on me. As the music blared, Ed shouted, "Move, move your body."

"I can't! I just can't. I'm so embarrassed!" I ran off the dance floor.

The big singles dances were started back in the late '80s, at some of the best suburban hotels on Sunday nights. I myself had disco fever and danced five nights a week. I became an excellent dancer, popular and even sexy. The guys would stand ten deep in line behind my chair waiting to dance with me. I became "the Belle of the Ball."

Not only was I dancing, I became a model and won second place in the Midwestern Modeling contest. I also had a lot of fun as an extra in the Hollywood movie *Double Dragon*, which was filmed in Cleveland, Ohio, featuring Alyssa Milano and Scott Wolf.

But by then, my dancing was really good. I'd started to enter contests and win. Tony became my dancing partner. I was very popular and my phone never stopped ringing. I gave 100 percent of my energy to my activities.

I met Barney, an older gentleman, at the dance. His wife had died earlier that year. In our conversation, he mentioned that he was looking for someone to live in his home to assist him; actually, he needed a housekeeper. He asked if I would be interested and might consider the position. I said I would give it some thought.

So, after much thought and a decision that took me six months to make, I finally accepted his offer and moved to Beachwood, a wealthy suburb of Cleveland.

Everything in life serves a purpose. At the time I accepted Barney's offer to live in his home, I would be helping him with his needs, and at the same time I'd be saving money for my retirement, since he offered free room and board. This changed over the years, and he asked me to share expenses of his home.

Totally unfair — it made me angry. I was responsible for duties around his house and also his wellbeing. Nevertheless, since I kept my office job, I was able to save money, and it was cheaper to pay Barney rent than pay expenses for an apartment. Actually, Barney's home felt like being in my own home, and I was very comfortable living there. My family was always welcome in his home, and so were all my friends; many times, there would be laughter and good conversation.

On occasion, Barney's children and grandchildren would visit. One particular visit was during my first Christmas at Barney's house. I happened to have a small Christmas tree that I'd planned to set up in the dining room. Now, Barney was Jewish, and I'm a Christian. When I told Barney about the tree, he yelled, "No, no, no, not in my house. What will my family think when they come for Hanukkah and see that tree?"

I replied, "What will my family think when they come for Christmas and see no tree? Well, then, I'll just put it into my bedroom window," I yelled, "and as the tree lights shine out into the night, into the street, everyone driving by will know we have a Christmas tree."

After much discussion back and forth, Barney said, "All right, Millie. Put the tree in the dining room."

"Are you sure?" I asked.

"Go ahead," he said. "We'll celebrate both Hanukkah and Christmas at the same time."

And so we did. Both families celebrated: what a joy it was. The thought of being together was accepted by everyone. The beauty of the tree captivated the little children, and they wished they could have a tree in their home for Hanukkah.

In months to come, there were many pleasant times in Barney's home, and times of disagreement. All in all, though, everything always worked out just fine.

During the week, my alarm clock would ring at 5 a.m. in order for me to get ready for my office job. One morning when I walked past Barney's room, I noticed his television was not on. Thinking he was tired, I let him sleep for a few more minutes. No, this was not right — Barney always woke up early to watch television. I returned to his room to wake him.

"Barney, are you all right?"

"Uh huh."

"Open your eyes."

"They are."

"No, they're not. Open them!"

"Hello, this is 9-1-1. What is your emergency?"

"Hello, I need an ambulance."

Barney had suffered a stroke, and was unable to recover from it. Six weeks later, he died. It just so happened that his son David gave me a gift of money, which compensated for the money I paid Barney in rent.

Seven years living with Barney had come to an end. At the time I accepted Barney's offer to be a housekeeper, little did I know that this position would lead me to a fantastic job offer in the future.

At that time, I was not aware of the future; I was only aware that I had to move from his home. So, another chapter in my life was now closed.

THE VISITOR

In the spring of 1993, I moved into my new apartment. A few weeks after I got settled, I took a nap one afternoon. As I awoke and was about to get up, I was conscious of what was happening, yet I could not open my eyes as hard as I tried, and my body fell into a paralyzed state. I could not move!

Suddenly, my kitchen door, which was locked, opened swiftly. My mother marched in, followed by eight to ten other ladies. All were smiling. They went from my kitchen, through the dinette area, into the living room, back past my kitchen, into the hallway, and out the door again, all in single file. It was as if I had x-ray eyes! I could see right through the bedroom wall as this was happening. My mother looked thirty years younger and very happy. She wore a beautiful blue dress, her hair was pulled into a bun, and she looked wonderful.

They marched quickly through my apartment. As soon as they left, I sat on the edge of my bed in disbelief at what just happened, and kept replaying in my mind what I'd just seen. For a few minutes, sudden fright overtook me, but after I calmed down, I realized my mother wanted me to see that she was well and happy, and also to let me know that she was watching over me, and was still with me.

How could I possibly tell anyone about this happening? Even I was in disbelief that something like this could happen — but it did happen, and it was real. Then I remembered the words my dad had spoken to me as a teenager: "There are heavenly beings or spirits around us." I remembered the comfort I felt in those words, and now I had experienced the spirit of my mother.

OLD MAN

One day I had a doctor's appointment. While I was sitting in the waiting room, an old man with a cane walked in slowly with difficulty, and I felt sorry for him. We were the only ones in the waiting room. I started to silently pray for him, asking God to give him relief from his pain.

After ten minutes of constant prayer, this man turned around and stared at me so intently that I was starting to feel uncomfortable. Then I realized he really felt the power of my prayer, and I hoped God gave him relief from his pain.

BURNED HANDS

One morning, my son George appeared in my dreams. He was holding out his arms and showing me the palms of his hands: his hands were burned, and the sleeves of his red-and-white checked flannel shirt had black burn marks on them. He said, "Mom, I got burned." The dream woke me up. I looked at the clock, and it was 5:30 a.m. The dream was so real to me. Later that morning, George called to tell me he had been lighting the pilot on the furnace and there was an explosion. He had burned his hand and had to go to the emergency room at the hospital. The accident happened at 7:30 a.m. that same morning.

WONDERS OF PRAYER

The year 1993 was a traumatic one for me. I had always said to God, "Put me where I should be at this time in my life. Let me do what you have planned for me, Lord."

It had been a year that I knew my office position would be phased out; now that time had arrived. By June, I was out of a job and had no income. Luckily I had money to pay the rent, and didn't have to pound the pavement looking for a job. Furthermore, I'd had my fill of working on a computer and longed to do another type of work. I knew that, sooner or later, I would have to start looking for employment, but at that time I had no ambition to do so. I really didn't know what the future held for me. I could only call upon God to bless me and show me the way I should go. Every day was filled with conversation and prayer with God.

Two months had gone by and my money was getting depleted. Then one day, the phone rang. When I answered, the voice asked "Millie Balas?"

I said, "Yes."

"This is Lloyd Schwenger. I have heard of you, and would like you to work for me."

Immediately, I knew that my prayers had been answered. This was the job I had been praying for. This is what God had planned for me.

Mr. Schwenger had heard of my work experience from a friend of his that had also known Barney. At our meeting, I was impressed with his 87 years, the quality of his lifestyle, and the goodness I saw within him. He was impressed that I knew how to cook. We bonded instantly. I became his housekeeper, and in time the salary was more than generous.

Now I knew what the future held for me. I also knew that God wanted me to help people.

Within two years, Mr. Schwenger developed dementia. I hired caregivers and took on more responsibilities for myself. I also became his companion, and his family wanted him to continue his social life. Many times we went to the Oakwood Country Club for lunch, or had dinner with his friends. At times, I would cook dinner for his friends and everyone would have an enjoyable evening.

The simple things in life brought him the greatest pleasure: his daily walks in the afternoon, going to Woolworth's at the mall, and having bacon and eggs for lunch. Perhaps they took him back to his youth and that is why they were pleasurable. Every now and then, we would have lunch with the boys. "The boys" were Mr. Schwenger's friends, some even from his childhood. The boys were in their late 80s and 90s.

Mr. Schwenger was an attorney and a wealthy, prominent person in the community. He loved his Jewish heritage and was involved with many organizations. His remaining family, his stepdaughter, Fran, his nephew, Paul, and niece, Pat, all lived out of town.

He truly was a gentleman from the old school, well-mannered and respectful towards others around him. His daily routine in the late afternoon was dressing in a suit for dinner and having a drink of vodka. We would then have dinner together. He would not leave the dining table until I was done eating, then we would nod to each other and both stand up to leave. Truly a gracious man.

I felt that Mr. Schwenger was very easy to get along with. We understood each other very well. At times, I felt like he was a father figure to me, especially when it came to money. I learned about the stock market, how to invest and make money. His family was wonderful to me when they would visit, especially Paul. He was like a son to Mr. Schwenger, and we always had a lot to talk about. Fran and Pat were enjoyable to be with, also.

Mr. Schwenger had a good life. I was with him for seven years, until September 2000. He lived to be 94.

You just know when God places you in a job. You know you belong, and you feel complete.

Chapter 6

Seasons

The seasons of my lifetime passed quickly. The new millennium — this long-awaited year of 2000 — was more than midway into the summer months. I looked back at my life and reflected over the days of my youth. I realized that I had been born in the last century, which now seemed so long ago. Suddenly this thought made me feel old.

On New Years Eve 1999, I prayed to receive God's blessing for the new millennium. I prayed for everyone in the family to have good health, joy, and the abundance of God's blessings. I prayed for the sick and the needy. I prayed for peace among humankind.

As I prayed, I thought and wondered what this new millennium would bring into my life. Where would my life's journey take me? I knew as the months unfolded I'd get a sense of what might lie ahead.

Our sons by now had families of their own. Ronnie married Karen in 1981, and was now 45 years old; Christopher, Matthew, and Megan were born to them. George had a daughter, Tara, from a previous marriage, and then, at the age of 41, was married to Eilene; she had two sons, Steven and Patrick, from a previous marriage. Leslie, two years younger than George, married and divorced and had remained single. Robert married Heather, and Logan was born. Robert, the youngest of the four brothers, was now 36 years old.

Our sons grew into manhood, became fine human beings, and had beautiful families. The brotherly love, the bonds between them were stronger than ever before.

Twenty-one years had passed since my divorce. That one particular winter day when Grandma Balas had called me and said, "I don't want you to be alone during Christmas," had then started a yearly tradition. The words she spoke that day were never forgotten. Her words swept us together as a family again.

The passing years were slowly beginning to show on Ron's face. His hair had turned silver-gray and had strands of white. He apologized and regretted the things he'd done during our marriage. Not only had his appearance changed, he showed humbleness and concern when he spoke.

Through the years, Ron kept in contact with his sons. He loved each and every one of them, and he was sorry he had missed out on a good part of their youths. His relationship with George was strained for several years. George's addiction to alcohol and his father not being there in his time of need caused the loss of togetherness. In later years, father and son developed a rapport and forgiveness.

George was a fantastic guy. He'd give you the shirt off his back if you needed it. But now the family felt he was the one who needed help: it was time for his addictions to stop. It was time for a family intervention. The family gathered at Eilene and George's apartment. George was surprised to see all of us that day. We explained why we'd come and expressed our love to him. We gave him words of support.

Robert's wife, Heather, was the person who was best able to reason with George. She had to keep fighting her own demons of addiction to prescription drugs, but she now showed surprising strength in the arduous task of convincing George to go for recovery. After several long hours of the family also reasoning with him, he was receptive to the idea. Everyone's face showed relief, as his recovery could now begin. We could all look forward to the future — not just for his wellbeing, but for all of ours. I thought I could now sense what the future had in store for me. I was in for a surprise.

One evening, I was relaxing and watching television, when suddenly I thought, *Whoa, what is wrong with me? I'm having heartburn — no, it's chest pain. Please, God, don't let me be having a heart attack. Oh my, gosh! Wow!* This was bad, and the pain was not going away. I had nothing in my apartment to soothe my pain, but finally I found a piece of peppermint candy that did the trick: my pain was gone. I thought if anything happened during the night I'd call 9-1-1, but for the time being, I was all right.

The next day, I felt fine and drove my friend Ida to the beauty shop. Ida happened to be 97 years old, and doing well health-wise. I worked a few hours per day to help her with chores. As I was driving her home again, a sharp pain occurred in my chest. "Ida, I think I'm having a heart attack."

"Oh, Millie, please just drive me home now," she said nervously.

I said, "Wait, it's just a sharp little pain. If it goes away, we'll stop at Jack's Deli for a quick lunch." The pain did go away, and we stopped for lox and cream cheese bagels with onion and tomato. Then I drove Ida home.

As soon as I got home, I called my doctor and made an appointment. Two days later, June 1 of 2001, I was in his office, and he ran an EKG. After reading the results, he came back to my room and said, "I already called an ambulance. Young lady, you're going straight to the hospital. Your EKG shows you had a heart attack." I was shocked at the outcome of my visit, then to be put into an ambulance and rushed to the hospital was too much to bear.

LIFE GOES ON

Three months had gone by since George went to the Interval Brotherhood Home in Akron, Ohio, and now he is being released. He called me a couple of days ago to ask if he could stay with me — Eilene had moved in with her sister, and their apartment was not big enough for all of them. I only had a one-bedroom apartment, but I said, "Sure, come on. We'll manage. You can sleep on the living room floor. Space will be limited, but it will work out fine."

The day I arrived at the hospital, George and Eilene came to see me. They bought me a gift: a small monster with angel wings. The doctor arrived and explained to all of us that I would receive stents in my arteries within the hour. My angioplasty procedure turned out fine, and after a one-week stay in the hospital, I returned home.

George was already there. He did everything he could to help me — he was so grateful that I'd allowed him to stay in my apartment. It took a few months for me to recuperate; the medications I was taking depleted my energy.

George was doing very well after he came home from IBH. He had put his addictions aside and tried to make the best of his recovery and his life. He and Eilene both worked at the Slovenian Home in the Collinwood area. He loved his maintenance job; he loved to work, and he felt proud of himself. He said he was feeling good. He had ten fingers and ten toes. "I'll make it, whatever I have to do in life."

Many times, Eilene would stay with us, and we would spend a lot of time talking. She was very religious, and we all had faith in the future.

When George came home from IBH he would have liked to stay with his father, but now he was staying at my place. At times, when we watched television, out of the blue George would remark, "Dad said he had no room for me. You said I could come and sleep on the floor." It was these unsettled thoughts that George had in his mind. Deep down he wished his dad would have said, "Yes, you can stay with me." Even so, he showed respect towards his father, but felt rejection at the same time.

George and I had interesting conversations. We talked about many things that had occurred in our lives. It seemed like his life was turning around for the better. Years of drinking had damaged his body. I had prayed for the day to come when he would stop; at last he was recovering, and I was so glad for him.

One particular conversation we had was about Grandma Ellis. Many times in the past years she had appeared in George's dreams. There were times when he could feel her presence beside him. He said that deep down he felt that Grandma was trying to tell him to stop drinking.

Even George was astonished to hear of my experience. I told him of the time Grandma's spirit had marched through my apartment with her spirit friends from Heaven. George and I both knew we could not talk to anyone about these happenings. Our conversation would not be believable to others. We both knew Grandma's spirit was with us, but I could see that George was troubled by his recurring dreams about Grandma, which would not go away.

LAZY SUMMER DAY

The days of the summer were hot, so George and I would go for a ride in my car. Sometimes we'd go back to his old neighborhood in Collinwood and visit one of his old haunts, Mirabile's. It truly was a place where everyone knew everyone else, including George. We would stop to have a delicious bowl of soup. Mirabile's was in a building that dated to the early 1900s. In the past years, factories in the community were booming with jobs, and Mirabile's thrived as the workers came in for lunch and supper. But now the factories stood empty, the workers long gone.

The restaurant and bar were old but well taken care of. Upstairs there were sleeping rooms — now in desperate need of repair — one huge bathtub in a room by itself, and one shower stall down the hall for all who lived there to use, at times including George.

It was now the month of August. Years had passed since Ronnie and Karen moved to Vermont, and now they have returned for a visit, bringing Megan and Matthew, who are now teenagers. Oh, what a wonderful treat for the family to be together once again, to laugh, talk, joke, and have cookouts.

When the boys were teenagers, I said to them, "Boys, you're all going to learn how to cook."

"What?"

"Ma, what are you doing to us?"

"I'm going to teach you how to survive."

"There aren't any bears here."

I said, "You have to survive no matter where you are. Listen, what if you never get married? Or what if you do, and later divorce?"

"What if, what if?"

"You've got to know how to cook!"

"All right, Ma, we know."

Well, soon they all started cooking and they have never stopped. To this day, they're all still cooking.

Now that the family was together again, Ron threw a couple of cookouts in his backyard. Of course, everyone came — no one wanted to be left out.

Over the years, the boys had acquired nicknames. George was now "Papa Georgio"; sometimes he was "Yogi Bear," so Eilene would become his sidekick, "Boo Boo." Leslie was called "Spatula" because he was always cooking. Robert was known as "Ziebart" because — just because. So when it came to cookouts, Papa Georgio would arrive and say, "Hey, Spatula, what you cookin'? Ziebart, don't eat everything up — leave some for me." The cooks were always clowning around and having a good time.

All the women brought their specialties, favorite foods and cakes from home to be served with whatever the guys were grilling at the time.

The family was together every day of Ronnie and Karen's vacation. Everyone had a marvelous time, but now it was time for Ronnie and his family to return to Vermont. Everyone was sorry to see them leave, and also to see the summer days slowly slipping away.

It was a September morning. I heard George while he was making coffee and getting ready for a new day. He was in the bathroom when I heard his frantic voice cry out, "Ma! Ma, come quick! I'm throwing up blood."

I jumped out of bed. "Oh my God," I yelled. "I'll call an ambulance."

"No, no — you drive me, Ma."

"Oh, my God, please help us!" I cried out.

"Drive me, *please*, Ma!" George pleaded with his voice. I threw on some clothes.

The two of us left the apartment to drive to Hillcrest Hospital, two blocks away. It took all my strength to get to my car with George. By now, he felt very weak and almost collapsed. I held onto him for dear life. I yelled at him, "Stand and walk! I can't hold you." We finally arrived at the hospital, and he was admitted to the ICU.

Eilene and I went to the hospital to be with George, to give him support, to give him comfort. He was doing much better the following day and he hoped to be released after a few days, but that evening the nurse called and asked if a member of the family could come to the hospital to calm George. He was out of control, in a state of confusion, relentlessly jumping up and down on his bed. I called his dad to go to the hospital to calm him.

The following day, the doctor had George transferred to the Cleveland Clinic. There he was heavily medicated and slept for many days. Fluid in his brain had caused his confusion, and he also had other problems. Eilene and I were by his side every day; it was a tedious and exhausting ordeal for both of us. After nearly thirty days, he recovered enough to go to rehabilitation.

One night, Eilene stayed at my apartment. Both of us were exhausted. At eight o'clock the next morning, my phone was ringing.

"Hello?"

"Ma! It's George. Open the door, buzz me in."

"Where are you, George?"

"Downstairs. Buzz me in."

"Okay," I answered with uncertainty.

Eilene asked, "Who called?"

"It's George. He's downstairs in the lobby. I just buzzed him in; he'll be here any minute."

In an anxious voice, Eilene said, "He hasn't been released from rehab. What are we going to do with him?"

"Stay calm, Eilene, be cool. We'll act normal, and let's be happy to see him when he comes upstairs." Both of us were nervous and didn't know what to expect.

George came into my apartment with a big smile on his face. We greeted him with hugs and kisses, at the same time flabbergasted by how he was dressed. He was wearing his shoes and pants, a paper hospital gown, and a blanket wrapped around his head and body. He looked like an Arab. I asked, "Why did you come home, George?"

"Oh, to take a shower and have breakfast," he answered. We knew he was still confused.

Eilene and I could not believe how he was able to come home; George had left his room at rehab, walked past the nurses' station on that floor, took the elevator to the main floor of the clinic, and walked out of the building. No one stopped him. No one questioned what he was doing. As a matter of fact, someone had even given him bus fare to ride the bus home. Once he got on the bus, the bus driver never questioned him or batted an eyelash. He just kept on driving.

How could this happen? Then it dawned on me — this must be an everyday occurrence. Someone is always walking out of rehab wearing hospital clothes, so the security guards on the premises and the bus drivers were used to seeing this. When George walked out wrapped in his hospital blanket, it was nothing unusual. At that time, I could not think otherwise.

This was a very unsettling matter. George took his shower and ate a good breakfast. Eilene and I drove him back to rehab at the clinic. George was totally unaware of his actions. By the time we arrived at the clinic, he was exhausted and unable to walk, so a wheelchair was provided to take him back to rehab.

HOME BEFORE THE HOLIDAYS

The long awaited day for George to come home from the clinic rehab had now arrived. He had taken good care of me during my illness, and I would now do the same for him. He was glad to be back in my apartment. He was glad that his ordeal of countless days of illness at the Cleveland Clinic was over.

A day did not end without my prayers. "Lift this burden of illness off my son, Lord. Fill his life with abundant health and wisdom. Let him be well and do what he should be doing. Thank you, Lord, for your blessings, your healing touch and guidance."

The holiday season was starting. I was not delighted. It was difficult to capture the holiday spirit with the health problems that had come upon us this year. I thanked God that we both survived. George, on the other hand, was delighted. He was still recovering, but looked forward especially to Christmas; this was his favorite holiday.

The week of Christmas, he went shopping. When he returned home, he was carrying a big box. "Mom, I bought you a tree. You can't have Christmas without a tree. Look, it's already decorated and it has lights. I even bought you a couple of little snowmen. Merry Christmas, Mom!" He gave me a big hug and a kiss.

"Oh, George, how sweet and thoughtful of you to do this." A feeling of warmth came into my heart as my mood for the season got lighter. After all, we'd spend this holiday together.

George had always worked, but now his health problems put him on disability. When his check arrived, he gave me money, not to spend, but to hold for his needs at a later date.

He was delighted preparing for this Christmas. It reminded me of times when he was a little boy. As I reminisced, I relived a Christmas past. How excited he would be, waiting for Christmas, especially for Christmas Eve and Santa to arrive. Then the magical hour would come. George and his brothers would anxiously wait and then watch, as the kitchen door slowly opened and in stepped Santa.

"Ho, Ho, Ho! Merry Christmas!"

"Ho, Ho, Ho, Merry Christmas, Saaan-ta."

"Grandpa? It's Grandpa Balas!" the boys would yell with excitement. "He's wearing his brown shoes. It's Grandpa. Grandpa, can we have our presents now?"

This year George was the Santa, as he then spent the rest of the day wrapping gifts for Eilene and Patrick and writing Christmas cards to everyone.

Christmas day arrived. The whole family gathered at Ron's house. Everyone was delighted to see George and glad that he was able to join in the holiday feast. Ron cooked a wonderful Christmas dinner: a big turkey, two ducks with all the trimmings, sweet potatoes, pumpkin pie, nut roll, and other favorite foods. It was always a good feeling to be together as a family. The closeness, love, and laughter would again make this a Christmas to remember.

DAWNING OF 2002

Another year was dawning, the year of 2002. So far the years of the new millennium had not been kind. During the past year with all the health problems, even I had to muster up enough strength just to cope with everyday tasks.

This would be the beginning of a better year. George's health was improving. Every day I prayed to receive God's blessing in our lives. I always thanked God for the blessings he had given me.

January was uneventful with its frigid weather and routine tasks. February was no different. George's mind was on the coming spring and being together once again with Eilene. He was getting restless living in my apartment. He slept in the living room; he had no place of his own, no privacy. He felt he didn't want to impose on me any longer, so he decided to move to a friend's house.

In the early spring while living there, he was doing spring cleanup in the yard when he was bitten on the arm by a spider. Again he had to be in the hospital for a week. He then came back to my apartment to recuperate.

It would only be one more month before George and Eilene would be living together again. Soon after his arm healed, he still wanted his own space, even if just for three or four weeks. George rented a room at Mirabile's. His father came over and pleaded with him not to go, thinking he might go back to his old habits and ways.

After he moved back to Mirabile's, George bought a bike, and he'd pedal over to his dad's house. One day, his dad cooked him a scrumptious meal of chicken paprikas. After being distant for many years, now it was just the two of them, and they had wonderful talks that brought them closer together. George raved many times about the dinner. Mostly he was very impressed that his dad took time to spend with him, especially since that was what he had really wanted for a very long time.

At times, Eilene and I would go to Mirabile's and we would all have lunch together. Other times, George and I would spend a day together. One day as I was driving, he asked, "Mom, do you still have the money I gave you at Christmas?"

"Yes I do, George."

"Okay, that's my dead money."

"What do you mean?"

"Ma, its dead money. I'll never be able to use it."

"Stop it, George! Don't call it *dead money*. Don't talk that way. What's the matter with you?"

I was quite upset by our conversation. I kept driving and nothing further was said.

The month of May arrived. It was time for Eilene's sister to move out and for George to move into their apartment. Eilene and George were happy to be together again, and to be able to do the things they loved to do.

Many times they went fishing at Daniel's Park. They would sit there for hours even if there was not a catch. It was the togetherness that was important.

One time they went to Lake Ladue. Roger, a friend of theirs, joined them for the day in the rowboat. They kept moving around on the lake, trying to find a good spot to fish. They were going to move again a third time, but Roger was rowing and rowing, and the boat would not budge.

George said, "Let me try." He rowed and rowed in circles.

Eilene said, "Fellas, you forgot to pull the anchor in. It's still in the water."

The B-2 Spirit Stealth Bomber was in Cleveland performing in the National Air Show. George and Eilene watched at a distance from a parking lot. They both wished they could have been closer. Later, they drove to their fishing spot. They walked to the bottom of a concrete embankment, where they could sit and watch for fish. Suddenly, a big shadow appeared in the water. George was not paying attention. Eilene said, "Look!" and their eyes moved from the water to the sky.

They could not believe what they saw, as the bomber was flying directly over them. George said, "Imagine that," while they watched in awe until it flew out of sight. The simple pleasures in life were always the best pleasures they both enjoyed.

George spent most of his time with Eilene. Once in a while, however, he could not resist the temptation to revisit his drinking buddies, and that cast a shadow over his future.

On Sundays they would go to church. Many times, friends would drop in to visit them at home, and George would offer them supper even though there was barely enough food in the house to feed the family. He had a wonderful heart. He always shared and gave to those in need.

One day I stopped to visit with George at his apartment. He'd never had a lot of possessions, but he had a large box holding a collection of memories, theater and concert tickets, mementos of places he had been with Eilene, his family and friends. In this box was a brooch, which had small turquoise stones. It had once belonged to Grandma Ellis. He had also saved the birthday cards she had sent him years before, and a Hungarian dictionary I had given him.

To my surprise, George said, "I want you to keep Grandma's brooch, and also this dictionary."

These items were precious to him, especially the brooch. Why would he be giving them to me? It seemed strange that he no longer wanted to keep them. He insisted that I should have them.

Chapter 7

Togetherness

It was already August. Ronnie, Karen, Megan, and Matthew came to visit again from Vermont. It was a most unusual summer; never in the past had everyone in the family gathered for picnics as we did that summer. Everyone thirsted for the closeness and love of the family. Everyone looked forward to doing things together. Many stories of past years were told at family get-togethers. Time after time, stories were repeated because they brought back fond memories. George would tell his favorite story often.

One day, Les and George stopped for a beer at a bar. On the way home, Les drove down Mayfield Road. He was going to take the shortcut through the Severance Center, but he happened to pass it. He quickly downshifted, the wheels spinning, the tires screeching as he quickly turned the car around and pulled into the Severance Center. Les remarked, "Whoa, we made it."

At the same time, three cop cars also made it, with their lights flashing; they immediately surrounded Les's car. George said, "Stay calm, be cool."

Les was mouthing off, though, and said, "I don't care what the cop wants. He can stick it up his —," not knowing that at the same time the cop was standing by his window and heard every word he said.

A big arm came through the window and grabbed Les by his shirt collar. It happened so fast that all George saw were Les's feet being dragged through the window as he exited from the car, then *click, click* went the handcuffs. The cop asked in a firm voice, "What's your problem, son?" This was always a funny story for everyone to hear.

Then Ronnie spoke up and asked, "Remember when Les saved coupons for Omaha Steaks? He received enough free steaks to feed everyone in the family that Christmas, and George and I grilled them on our front porch."

"Yeah, that was a wonderful Christmas dinner," replied Les.

Ronnie said, "Oh, I have a good story. What about the time my friends and I were cruising the neighborhood in a car? We just happened to have a mannequin's leg in the car. As we cruised, we put the leg out the window. Passersby went crazy; they didn't know what to think when they saw this leg going up and down in the window. They thought it was real."

Les said, "You did some crazy things, Ronnie."

George spoke up and said, "One of the best picnics you can attend is the Hungarian Fall Festival. It's a traditional event; bunches of grapes are hung from the rafters over the dance floor, and as everyone dances, people steal the grapes. The men, especially, would grab bunches for their wives or girlfriends. If a cop caught you stealing, you would go to jail right there, in a cage in the woods. Of course, it's all in fun, and you try not to get caught, but if you do get caught you're soon released. Then you could go back to steal more grapes."

Growing up, Robert had missed out on a lot of antics with his brothers because he was too young, but not anymore. It was fun to steal the grapes, get caught, and meet his brothers in jail.

The whole family always attended the picnics, not only to enjoy the tradition, but also the heritage of our ancestors. The family's togetherness was a marvelous way to end the days of August. Ronnie, of course, could not go back to Vermont without seeing his favorite baseball team, the Cleveland Indians, and plenty of hotdogs were eaten that night.

It was time for Ronnie and his family to return home. The reminiscence of by gone days had been enjoyable.

Everyone was brought up-to-date with the current happenings in each of our lives, and we all hoped to be together again next year.

During this trip, Ronnie took pictures so that he could savor memories of the vacation after they returned to Vermont. At one of the cookouts, Ronnie realized he might not see George again for a long time. He saw that he had only one shot left in his camera. He yelled out, "Hey, George!" and George waved back at him as Ronnie snapped his picture. Little did Ronnie know that it would be the last picture of George waving goodbye.

DOWNTOWN

One of the nicest days I had in August in the summer of 2002 was with my son George. He called to tell me that his truck needed repair, and asked if I would pick him up at the repair shop because it would take a few hours to fix.

I met George at the repair shop, and we decided to have lunch. There was a diner on East 55th Street that George wanted to go to. We drove down Euclid Avenue to get to the diner and passed the Cleveland Clinic, where George had spent several weeks very ill the previous year while recovering from his addictions. I said "Thank God you're not there."

He replied, "Thank God."

As we drove on, I was in awe of the beautiful new buildings on Euclid Avenue and enjoyed the ride. As we drove farther into the inner city, however, the streets took on a worn out, decrepit appearance. Amidst all this, we arrived at the diner, which was attractive and clean. The clientele surprised me — mostly businessmen, not quite what I'd expected to see. The food was great, and we had an enjoyable lunch.

After lunch, we decided to go downtown. As we drove along the lakeshore, the sun was glistening brightly and dancing on the waves of Lake Erie. We passed Burke

Lakefront Airport and drove down to the pier by the USS Cod, got out of the car, and walked around. We passed Jacobs Field and also saw some beautiful gardens. As I looked over at George, I saw the exhilaration on his face, and his smile as he said, "If it was my choice, and if I could afford it, I'd live in the city." He loved the excitement, sights, sounds, smells, and bustle of the people.

It was finally time to go to pick up his truck. As we said goodbye I had a peaceful feeling, and was glad that we had shared a wonderful day. Being with George brought back nostalgic memories of when I was a young girl and my mother took me downtown on the streetcar; we would go to the May Company, Higbee, the dime store, and Clark's Restaurant, and these memories were treasures in my mind. This adventure was with my son — something we had never done before — and as it was happening, I savored every moment. Little did I know that we would never do this again, and this would also become a treasure in my memory.

THE FAVORITE CONCERT

The days of summer were now over. Monday night, October 4, a Paul McCartney concert would be the main attraction in Cleveland. Les had purchased tickets, and he invited George to go with him.

"We sure had good times listening to The Beatles when we were growing up," said George. "Here we are, years later, at Paul McCartney's concert. Les, this is the best concert I've ever gone to in my life. I'm glad you invited me to come along."

George loved music. In days gone by, many times he would sing along with songs he heard on the radio. He had a beautiful tone in his voice when he sang. I wished I would have known about his talent when he was younger, but I just now discovered it.

****

****

Heavenly Father, on bended knees I cry out to thee with the anguish that now surrounds me.

****

****

Chapter 8

Destiny

THE FATAL STEP

October's glorious colors of the trees and the splendor of life amid the autumn leaves bring thoughts of what life could have been — but now is not, as the stillness of life has come.

And so it was: my beloved son George passed away. Such grief I had never known. Although time heals the heart, the haunting reality always remains with you, with the thoughts of what could have been.

October 21st was an ordinary Monday. I could not foresee what the day had in store for me. In the latter part of the afternoon, I received a phone call from my son Les. He called to tell me that George had lost his footing and fell on some stairs. He was taken to Euclid General Hospital. Within an hour, Les called again to tell me that George had been put on life support, and was being Life Flighted to Akron General's Trauma Center. Akron was the only trauma center that had space for George.

Les, George's wife, Eilene, and I drove to Akron, Ohio. By the time we arrived, it was after 9 p.m. George's father, his brother Robert, and his wife, Heather, had already arrived and were waiting for us. After a quick discussion, George's brother Ronnie was notified in Vermont; he arrived a couple of days later with his children, Matthew and Megan. We talked and prayed, and then proceeded down the corridor to the ICU.

As we entered my son's room, I was shaken. I kissed his forehead and held his hand. I cried while his seemingly lifeless body lay in bed. I prayed and pleaded to God, "Only you can heal him, Lord. Please don't take my son." But as I prayed, my hopes and anticipation for his recovery were fading. I told my son I loved him.

I pondered why this had happened. Why was I not forewarned, like I had been of my mother's death? I asked God for an answer. There was only silence.

The following day, Tuesday, there was no change in George's condition. The doctor was amazed that George was still alive. He said, "Patients don't live this long after a head trauma such as his." Eilene and Heather stayed overnight to keep vigil and pray.

It was now early Wednesday morning. As I got into Les's truck, we greeted each other, "Good morning."

I looked at Les; he seemed very quiet, and his manner was reserved. I asked, "Are you okay?"

Immediately, he said, "Mom, I have to tell you what happened to me in the early hours of this morning."

"What happened?" I became concerned. What could have happened?

Les kept driving. He said, "We have to get to the hospital as soon as possible." I looked at his face, which now showed sadness and concern. At times, as Les spoke, he would pause his words as tears filled his eyes. My eyes also filled with tears while I listened to every word he spoke; my mind was enthralled, and I was in complete awe. I sat in total silence as Les told me what had happened to him early that morning.

I will now share with the reader Les's spiritual journey with his brother George, in his own words as he revealed it to me.

THE SPIRITUAL RAPTURE OF HEAVEN

October 23, 2002: Early morning — I estimate probably between four and five o'clock in the morning — I found myself in an area that I was very unfamiliar with. Uh — it was a place of white, the most beautiful color white that you can possibly imagine. I couldn't tell how far or large this area was. I couldn't tell if this beautiful shade of white ended at the tip of my nose or went on for miles.

I found myself very comfortable, assured, not worried about my surroundings, but feeling very comfortable and warm in this area I was in. Uh..., how long I was there is very, very hard to figure out; I couldn't tell you if I'm there for an hour, or if I'm there for two minutes. But, Uh..., next thing I know, I find myself — that I need to turn around, just turn to the right, and so I did. I don't know where this voice came from, or if something in my head told me to turn.

I found myself on my knees with my hands clasped together in front of me, looking down. At this point in time, again, no matter which direction I looked, it was the most colorful or most beautiful color of white you could possibly imagine. This point in time something, Uh..., *told* me I could look up, to see what's in front of me. And as my head slowly rose and my eyes glanced upward, there was George. The most unbelievable sight I — I could possibly imagine.

The atmosphere around him, Ah..., I just burst out and said, "George, my God — you look beautiful," then realizing that my mouth is not moving, like a telepathy-type communication.

The aura around him, the radiance, his hair — no blemishes, everything was perfect, just beautiful. The clothes that he wore were like a light grayish, very formfitting uniform. He was standing in an area where there appeared to be possibly some type of arch. But, again I couldn't tell how far behind him things were — but there was definitely some type of outline of this area he was in.

Again I said, "George, I can't believe how beautiful you look." And with his eyes, my eyes

— we never broke eye contact....this meeting that took place.

He said to me, "Les, you can't imagine what I feel. There's no way on earth that you could possibly comprehend how I feel right now. The love — there's no pain — the happiness," and as he's communicating this to me, he has a tremendous smile on his face, and the radiance, the glow all about him, the aura around him. Ah..., I realized that I could not get any closer to him.

I was probably a distance of about twelve feet — ten to twelve feet — away and something told me that I could not get any closer, this was as close as I probably could go, and, uh, we communicated just the same things over and over, just how beautiful, the love, the happiness, no pain, no suffering.

At this point, something told me I had to look down, and doing so, I noticed I couldn't see George's feet, nor could I see mine, uh..., just on my knees with my hands clasped in front of me. I'm looking down and I just gazed at my hands and the whiteness of possibly a floor beneath me, or I don't know what it was, but again the most beautiful color of white you could possibly imagine.

At this point in time, something told me I could look up again, which I did slowly — lifted my head and gazed in front of me, and George was no longer there.

Um..., finally, I found that I could stand back up and I could be in this room for I don't know how long it was. I couldn't tell you — again, two minutes, two hours — but the next thing I remember, I was in my bed in a sit up position, with my eyes open and my jaw dropped, and I said three words. There were three words that came out of my mouth, and they were, "Oh, my God!"

It was pitch black in my apartment. I found myself starting to cough, tremble, and shake uncontrollably — and that happened. I felt that experience for the next twenty minutes, almost bouncing out of bed, shaking, trembling, coughing to the point of exhaustion... and that finally did subside.

Still pitch black in the apartment, I remember getting out of bed, walking into the kitchen, opening the cupboard and reaching for a glass, turning on the water, and taking a few sips of water. Pitch black. I have no idea how I navigated my way around the apartment at that point in time, but I found myself back in bed, crawled back in and slept for a short period of time, to be awakened by the telephone.

It was roughly around 6 a.m. by then, uh...and to be awakened by the telephone — it was Robert calling me to get dressed. "Don't take a shower, just pick up Ma and get down to Akron General as fast as you possibly can."

We got down there to find that George's, Um..., his vitals had dropped drastically and they're going to have to pull him off life support.

I believe that George came to me and took me to an area that no earthly human being can venture to. It was a unique experience. No earthly being is supposed to be in that area, but I believe George somehow pulled a few strings, brought me there to let me know that his time had come and that he was all right.

And I'll never forget this experience as long as I live. I'm sure I'll see this area again when the time comes; with the love that George and I had for each other, the times that we had together, he just wanted me to know that he was okay and that

he's in a better place. God bless you, George. I
love you.

Sometimes there are no words to express our thoughts.
Words escaped my mind as Les revealed his awesome
spiritual rapture to me. He appeared almost angelic while he
spoke. The beauty of his experience overwhelmed me with
tears of joy. "Ooh, Les, you've given me the chills. You had
a spiritual out-of-body experience. You crossed over and
reached the gates of Heaven. George gave you the message
of love to strengthen you and to let you know he is well. My
God, Les — what a blessed experience you had."

When we arrived at the hospital, we both knew that
George was no longer with us. As I prayed, a sense of peace
came over me. I could not hold back my tears, as I longed for
life to be the way it once had been when my son George was
around me.

When Ron arrived, he was caught up in overwhelming
grief. He reflected on his own life and sensed the loss of time
he'd never savored with his son.

The following day was Thursday. The hours passed
slowly. The minister led my family in prayer, and as we
prayed, the pieces of mechanical equipment were turned off
one by one. Then the life support equipment was unplugged.
Not another breath was taken — not even one. And as the
curtain in the room was drawn around the bed, I said, "God
love and bless you, son."

And as the stillness of his life has come, his legacy of
love remains in our hearts.

REMEMBERING SPECIAL TIMES

"I have ten fingers and ten toes. I'll make it, whatever I
have to do in life!" George said.

"Wake up, George!" said Ronnie when he first saw him
in the ICU. "We always did everything together."

"Ronnie, let's go to the bakery for a donut after we deliver these newspapers."

"Hey, Spatula. What are you cooking? Ziebart, don't eat everything up. Leave some for me."

"Mmm, Dad, the chicken paprikas you made is delicious."

"Eilene, let's get up early to go fishing, then later in the morning we'll go to church."

"Mom, I bought you a Christmas tree. You can't have Christmas without a tree."

"Oh, Les, the Paul McCartney concert was the best concert I've ever gone to in my life."

PREMONITION

In the months preceding George's death, there were strange moments, as if he knew something was going to happen. He seemed to be preparing for his own death.

For years, George had possessed Grandma Ellis's brooch, and of course the attachment of sentimental feelings — yet he gave her brooch to me and insisted I keep it.

The Sunday before his accident, George's behavior was most unusual. He owned two suits and had worn them several times. That afternoon, he went into the bedroom to try them on. He asked Eilene, "Which one looks the best on me? That's the one I want to go to church in."

Eilene said, "Services were over two hours ago."

Weeks after George gave me money to hold for him at Christmas time, he started to call it his "dead money." It was this money I used to pay for his funeral expenses.

Ronnie felt a strange sensation when he looked at the photo he had taken of George three months earlier. George was waving goodbye, as if to say *farewell*.

```
************************************************
************************************************
```

The following are occurrences that happened shortly after George's death.

```
************************************************
************************************************
```

Chapter 9

The Spirit

THE MESSAGE

About two weeks after my son George died, he came to me in a dream. It appeared he was out in space, in a large spiral tunnel that had a purplish hue. Outside the tunnel, it was dark, yet light enough for me to see. George was walking toward me with a young man. George stopped and his friend stepped aside. George said, "Mom, you are well."

They both wore checked flannel shirts. His friend was tall, thin, and had sandy brown hair. As I looked down at George's feet, I saw green blades of grass surrounding the spiral. I awoke immediately and knew this truly was a message.

In the next few weeks, I would be tested for cholesterol. I would also have a Pap smear test. The cholesterol results were very good, and my cardiologist was pleased.

My Pap test the past two years had shown foreign cells. Although I'd had two surgical procedures, the problem did not go away. My gynecologist insisted that I should consider a hysterectomy, but I wanted a second opinion and went to see another doctor.

In December I had another Pap test. I told the new doctor about the dream I'd had, and that I was well. The doctor just looked at me, and didn't know what to say other than that the tests would give the results.

My test results came back clean. My doctor wanted me to take another test in three months to make sure the test results were correct. The test came back clean every three months for a year. The doctor was assured that the tests were clear and okay.

I knew George loved me very much. He appreciated everything I did for him. I thank God for my healing. I thank George for bringing me the message.

We are rewarded for the good deeds we do unto others, not just by people here on earth, but also beings from beyond.

OUR GANG ON REDWOOD

We had wonderful neighbors when our sons were growing up, one of whom was Lois. Her son Bob was Ronnie's age, and during the summer they would be together almost every day, building go-carts. George and Les, both much younger, would help them build these go-carts.

At the time of George's death, I called Lois and said I'd send her pictures of remembrance from when the boys were young. So I did, and wrote the caption "Our Gang on Redwood" on the photos.

I mailed the photos at the post office, then proceeded to drive to the grocery store. I tuned into 100.1 FM on the radio, Howie Chizek's talk radio show. To my surprise, Howie and a female caller were having a conversation about our gang — the Little Rascals.

This woman was describing one of the Rascal movies she had seen. The rascals were all in the bathroom; the shower curtain was covered with comic characters. When the gang pulled the shower curtain back, there stood George.

I could not believe what I was hearing. Of all the movies the Little Rascals made, they were talking on the radio program specifically about this one particular film, *Our Gang*, and it was none other than George behind the shower curtain.

Was this an uncanny coincidence, or was I meant to hear it on the radio? To say the least, I was quite shaken by this experience.

A Spirit Revealed

Every day, my thoughts turn to George. In January 2003, I parked my car in the garage. It was early evening, after work, about 6:30 p.m. I proceeded to walk to my apartment building. As I walked past another apartment building, I heard a rustling in the bushes. The sound startled me, sending chills down my spine. Then I heard fast running, like some kind of animal; it ran as if it was trying to outrun me, or that I should definitely take notice of this creature. Suddenly, it took off into the air. Darkness had fallen. I thought it was a wild turkey: it appeared to be very large, and the bird, whatever it was, flew to the top branches of a tree in the parking lot.

In all my years of living, I've never experienced anything like this. I instantly felt George's presence, his energy. It overcame me with a powerful feeling of anxiety.

Two weeks later I was driving my friend Nancy home to Shaker Heights. As I was pulling into her driveway, she asked, "What is that big thing in the tree?" I backed the car up to see what it was. A huge gray-and-white owl was sitting in the tree. Nancy said, "All the years I've lived in Shaker Heights, I have never seen an owl." I had a strange feeling that George was letting me know he was watching over me, and that he was okay.

Grandpa's Death And The Owl

Early morning on January 27, 2004, my father-in-law passed away. Dad was Grandpa to his grandchildren, and there was lots of love between them.

While I was praying on January 29th, I was looking out my bedroom window. Across from my window, a bird landed on a tree and interrupted my prayers. I stared at this bird, because it looked different than other birds. I grabbed my binoculars to get a better look: it was an owl — a gray-and white owl — probably the same owl that had appeared after George passed away.

I stopped praying; my interest was completely absorbed by the owl. I stood looking out the window, staring at him. I'd never seen an owl except in the country, but as strange as it seems, it appeared to me again as it had after George's death. I just thought how precise the timing of this owl's appearance was. I finally stopped watching it and left the window. I went back to this window later, but the owl was gone. I felt his message: Grandpa was all right.

PENNIES FROM HEAVEN

My heart was filled with sorrow as I grieved over George. I talked to him every day. At times, I wanted to know if he was around me. I asked him to send me pennies.

Two weeks went by; nothing happened. Then early one morning, I was walking by my apartment on the sidewalk toward my car. When I came to the end of the walk, I was amazed to see several hundred pennies lying in the grass. I scooped up as many as I could into a bag. The following day, I went to the laundry room and found five pennies on the floor. Two days later, I went to the mall to look for a dress that would fit me. I found one, and went to the dressing room to try it on; the dress fit perfectly. In front of the mirror, on the floor, was a penny. I said, "Thank you, George!"

During the weeks that followed, I said to George, "If you are here, send me a penny." Since then, I have found several pennies.

THE FUNERAL

On Saturday, January 31, 2004, the day of Grandpa's funeral, I was going to Eilene's car, and found a penny by her back tire.

After the funeral, the family gathered in my apartment building's party room for refreshments. Later, several family members also came to my apartment. Another penny was found almost in front of my door. Could it be that both George and Grandpa were with us?

A SUNNY DAY

On Wednesday, October 1, 2003, I was looking out of my bedroom window and talking to God. I was looking at the sky as I asked God to give me a sign to let me know if my son George was all right. I stood by the window for a couple of minutes, but nothing happened, so I went to watch television.

On *Good Morning America*, George Lopez was filling in as the weatherman for Tony Perkins, whose wife had a baby. As I sat down, the national weather map was on the screen, and only cities named "George" were shown on the map. I could not believe what I was seeing — Wow! What a sign. I was meant to see this.

MEANT TO BE

During the joyous holiday season, Eilene, George's widow, joined her family at their church for a holiday program. Upon leaving, her spirits were crushed when she discovered that her car had been stolen from the church's parking lot.

After filling out a police report and waiting several days for the car to be found, she realized that she needed transportation and had to buy another car immediately.

The search for a car began; after looking at a few, she saw a red car in excellent condition, a Prizm. Unfortunately, the owner would not come down on his price, and the car was already ten years old. This car would be reliable transportation for her.

As much as Eilene wanted this car, nothing was happening in her favor. Eilene was having difficulties securing a bank loan, and, to make matters worse, she came down with the flu and was stuck in the apartment until she felt better. Because she had no transportation, she was unable to get to work.

Eilene had always been a very spiritual person, so she began to pray. Within a few days, the man with the Prizm called Eilene to let her know he would come down in price for the car, and would also fix the brakes for her. Eilene felt her prayers had been answered, especially when the bank called to let her know that her loan application was approved.

The radio station Eilene always tuned into was 95.5 FM, called the FISH station — no nasty words or bad lyrics. The owner of the Prizm picked Eilene up and took her to the bank to finalize the loan. You see, this man was also of good character and perhaps spiritual: his car's radio was tuned to 95.5 FM. Eilene discovered this when she turned on the radio, and instantly she knew in her heart that the car was meant to be hers.

A few days later, she found a penny in the back, on the floor of the car. It was George leaving his trademark, and letting her know that he knew about the car.

AND THIS WAS GEORGE

George had a very close relationship with Eilene's family. When her sister Marge was in hospice, he would go and sit with her. The New Year's Eve before her death, he wanted to visit her; around 11:59 p.m., Eilene and George entered her room. Even though she was sleeping and was not aware of their presence, they sat with her for a little while so that she would have someone to bring in the New Year with her.

In the past, if George had something on his mind, he could always talk to Marge. If he borrowed money from her, he always insisted on paying her back as soon as he was paid, as he did with everyone. When Marge died, George was torn, and couldn't attend the services.

When George died, Karen, a niece of Eilene's, told a little story. She said that she could see George going up to heaven and meeting up with Marge and her husband. After they'd said their hellos, he took Marge aside and made a request. "Marge, could I borrow some of your angel dust? I haven't earned mine yet, and I need some to sprinkle on Eilene and Patrick."

****

****

During our lifetimes on this earth, life can reveal amazing experiences. Mysteries and unexplained events can occur. We may ponder what the essence of life is. Ultimately, in time, the glory of the spiritual rapture of Heaven will be revealed to all of us.

****

****

PSALMS 23:1–6

The Lord is my shepherd; I shall not want.

He maketh me to lie down in green pastures: he leadeth me beside the still waters.

He restoreth my soul: he leadeth me in the paths of righteousness for his name's sake.

Yea, though I walk through the valley of the shadow of death, I will fear no evil: for thou art with me; they rod and they staff they comfort me.

Thou preparest a table before me in the presence of mine enemies: thou anointest my head with oil; my cup runneth over.

Surely goodness and mercy shall follow me all the days of my life: and I will dwell in the house of the Lord for ever.

AMEN

Epilogue

Before the foundation of the earth, God had a purpose and plan for each of our lives. Do you believe in destiny? Each of us was predestined and chosen for such a time as this. This book is a powerful true story of the joy and pain that a family experiences. Every chapter reveals how the presence of God was in each and every circumstance in their lives.

Ron and Matilda Balas married, had children, and — after the worst stages of their relationship ran their courses — peace again surrounds them. Through the years of trials and tribulation, Ron and Matilda have gained an understanding of each other and of themselves. Both are active in functions that involve their family.

I give God all of the praise, honor, and glory. I thank Him for the opportunity and revelations He gave me while working on this project. I am blessed to know and be a friend of Matilda Balas and her family. It is not by chance that our paths crossed in this life, for it was predestined before the foundation of the earth. Love endures forever.

— Reaitta Irby

"In whom also we have obtained an inheritance, being predestinated according to the purpose of him who worketh all things after the counsel of his own will: That we should be to the praise of his glory, who first trusted in Christ."

(KJV Ephesians 1:11-12)

****
****

The prayers are still being answered. The most current blessing occurred at Our Lady of Lourdes Shrine and Grotto, November 4, 2005.

****
****

Our Lady of Lourdes Shrine

The Blessing

The day was November 1, 2005. I was awakened by the daylight streaming through my window. There was no need to rush; this would be a restful day, and later I would have lunch with a friend. I had no clue what my day would really be like, nor did I know that today's events would culminate by the end of the week into spiritual knowledge. The bounty of love and spirituality would manifest itself at Our Lady of Lourdes Shrine and be shown to me.

Suddenly, I was startled to see what appeared to be a huge black cobweb forming within my left eye. I had just applied my mascara — perhaps some had gotten into my eye. When I looked into the magnifying mirror, my eye looked clear even though I still saw the cobweb. I quickly realized the problem was within my eye, and I began to panic. Soon I was petrified, as I lost my sight for a few seconds. I called out, "Please, God — please, God, bring back my sight!"

Finally, I could see the cobweb shredding apart, and within ten minutes this awful invasion was disappearing. I was able to see better, and I regained my composure. I immediately went to the doctor; after a thorough examination, I left his office with a brief explanation and a pamphlet that did little to ease my fear.

On Friday, November 4, 2005, I awoke and felt disappointed that my eye was not better. I was very worried. Would my vision be impaired? Could I lose my sight? I said my morning prayers and told God that I needed answers. Within the hour, I received an unexpected phone call from a friend that gave me the answers. Then I experienced an overwhelming desire to be at the Our Lady of Lourdes Shrine. No matter how hard I tried, I could not shake this overpowering feeling within me. The spiritual experience I was about to encounter would go beyond anything I have ever experienced.

Our Lady of Lourdes Shrine

November 4, 2005

During the years I was growing up, I remember singing a song in school, in which the words described a tree in all its beauty and glory. It went on to say that only God can make a tree. These words stayed with me, and I began to take notice of things God can do.

This morning I could hardly contain my joy: I received an answer to my prayer. Knowing my eye would be all right, I was bursting with joy and felt compelled to go to the Our Lady of Lourdes Shrine. I've been there in the past to light a candle in remembrance of my son George. On the way to the shrine, I had to pass Richmond Mall. I had no intention of going there, but soon realized that I had parked my car and was at the mall, as if the car had driven itself. Since I was there, I decided to take a walk in the mall.

After my walk, I was anxious to be on my way. I drove down the hill on Chardon Road to the Our Lady of Lourdes Shrine. As I walked to the Grotto, I passed the chapel and the gift shop. In the summer months, the paths to the Grotto are adorned with scented roses, cosmos, snapdragons, and lush greenery. Today, the paths were bare; the season for flowers to bloom had passed. It was Friday, November 4, 2005. The skies were gray, yet there was enough warmth to feel comfortable. Once inside the alcove of the shrine, I lit candles in thanksgiving for the answers to my prayer earlier that morning. I also lit a candle in memory of my son George. I walked out into the Grotto and sat down to pray by the statue of Our Blessed Lady. In the stillness of my surroundings, I stared at her as I meditated. A feeling of euphoria came over me, and it brought joy to my heart. I felt comfortable being there, and stayed for a while.

When I stood up to leave, I noticed a nun sitting at the back of the Grotto. I felt compelled to talk with her and approached her while she was saying the rosary.

"Sister, may I sit down?"

"Please, do. I'd love to have you join me."

I introduced myself as Matilda; she was Sister Clara. Holding her rosary, she told me she always made the Stations of the Cross in the chapel. Today, she did not know the reason why she'd come to the Grotto. "Sister Clara, I have a reason. I had an overwhelming desire to be here today; even so, on my way here, I can't explain why I stopped at the mall." As we spoke, I realized how precise the timing of this meeting was. If I had come sooner, we would not have met.

"Our meeting was meant to be," said Sister Clara. We both felt divine intervention had brought us together. "What brings you here today Matilda?"

"I'm not Catholic," I said. "I'm spiritual, and often come to light candles in remembrance of my son. This morning, I received an answer to my prayer, and came to light a candle of thanks."

"Sister Clara, a few days ago I had a frightful experience. I saw what appeared to be a cobweb forming, and then shredding apart, within my left eye; it caused my sight to disappear for several seconds. My doctor gave me a thorough exam. He explained how the vitreous gel had pulled away from the back wall of my eye, leaving floaters that impaired my vision. This morning, I awoke feeling disappointed because my eye was not better. I said my prayers and told God that I needed answers. I later called my doctor for more in-depth answers, but he was busy and unable to talk, and would call me back.

"Then, Sister Clara, something unusual happened: within minutes, I received an unexpected call from my friend Franny in California. I had not talked to her in months. Our conversation was beyond my expectations, as she spoke of her recent eye surgery. Her problem was worse than mine, and she is doing fine. I began to feel better while she spoke of her experience, and she was able to answer my questions. She said there was no need to worry about surgery if my retina was intact, which it is; I will not lose my sight, and my eye will be fine.

"I said to her, 'Franny, this morning I prayed and asked God to give me answers. You just gave them to me.' As we said goodbye, I'm not sure if she believed what I said, but I knew my prayers had been answered and I would be fine. Sister, within minutes my phone rang again. It was my doctor calling. 'I'm late returning your call,' he said. 'I tried, but could not get through. My girl gave me the wrong phone number.'"

"Matilda, everything happens for a reason. God works in mysterious ways and gives us answers through other people. Franny was the messenger." Sister Clara then spoke of the shrine's history.

"Many healings have taken place at this shrine, Matilda. God uses the water to manifest His healing love. Visitors from all parts of the world have come to pray and request their petitions. The Good Shepherd Sisters acquired this property in 1920. During a visit in 1922 to their motherhouse in France, they visited the world famous shrine in Lourdes. They were given a small piece of stone from the rock where the Virgin Mary stood when she first appeared to Bernadette in 1858, and this stone has been divided into three pieces. Water flows over one small piece below the statue of Our Blessed Lady. Many healings have been attributed to drinking of this water. Another piece of the stone is embedded into a prayer book. The third piece is in a repository at the gift shop."

Sister Clara went on to say, "Don't forget to pray, Matilda. Pray to the Holy Mother, and she will see that your prayers are answered."

I mentioned to Sister Clara that the sun was shining as I glanced up and saw a pale yellow sun. Even though her back was turned to it, she simply said, "Yes, I know."

We talked about many things. My mind was flooded with spiritual inspiration. Even though we'd just met, I was pouring out my deepest thoughts and feelings from within my heart. The spiritual bond between us was immediate. Sister Clara was very gracious, with many words of wisdom to share with me.

The afternoon hours were quickly slipping away. The time was nearing 5 p.m. Sister Clara had duties to perform and had to leave. "Before you go, Sister Clara, please say a prayer for me."

She stood up, embracing my face with her hands. Her beautiful prayer inspired me, and I was unable to control my tears. I happened to glance up and noticed the strange appearance of the sun: the pale yellow sun was no longer shining; it had become bright orange and was surrounded by the gray sky. When I looked up again, the sun had become a deep orange color, as if a thin veil was covering its brightness. The beauty of the sun was mystical. I knew I was looking at something I'd never seen before, yet I didn't realize the significance of what had occurred.

Our inspirational meeting was ending. I walked partway to the convent with Sister Clara. "In my lifetime, my prayers have been answered many times, Sister Clara. I'm writing a book about my spiritual encounters."

"You must let me read it, Matilda."

Driving home, I pondered the day's inspirational feeling within me. I stopped for a red light, and a message on the license plate of the car in front of me read, "LT IT B." I knew everything was in God's hands. This had been a powerful spiritual day for me. I felt as if I experienced a day in the infinite realm of the spiritual world. Only later would I realize how privileged I had been.

I had to share this day's experience with my friend Reaitta. She had been working on my manuscript, and we share a spiritual bond. Until we spoke, unbeknownst to me, the beautiful mystic sun had also been revealed to her. Reaitta was at work that day, sitting at her desk; a few moments before 5 p.m., a strong impulse lead her to the window. She was astonished to see the sun radiating with such beauty, and could not stop looking at it. This was no coincidence. Reaitta and I were miles apart when this happened. God's timing was precise. Just before 5 p.m., during Sister Clara's prayer, we both witnessed this array of heavenly beauty. On that day, I spoke to Reaitta. We realized the two of us were spiritually bonded; in that moment of time the sun revealed its splendor to both of us, on that very special Friday in November.

I immediately wrote a letter to Sister Clara. I expressed my heartfelt thanks and fondest thoughts to her, along with this question, "Please, Sister Clara, explain the significance of the sun on November 4th." Her prompt response to my letter and the magnificence of that day brought me to tears.

The Letter

My Dear Matilda,

With heartfelt pleasure, I respond to your gracious letter, received today as November 15.

It was a pleasure to hear from you, as I kept you in prayer and reviewing in my mind all that took place on November 4th.

Matilda, that day was meant to be, since I usually make the Stations of the Cross in the Chapel, but decided on the 4th to make them outside.

So, having done so, I decided to sit outside facing the Grotto to say my rosaries. Then our beautiful time began, as we expressed our past, and present, as it was meant to be. Our Blessed Lady knows how and when, and to whom, to make manifest miracles and blessings. That day She gave you many blessings.

Now, Matilda, this is about the sun and what you saw on Nov. 4th.

On October 13, 1917, Our Lady of Fatima told children God would work a miracle on that day so that all would believe; 70,000 people saw it.

In 1942, Pope Pius XII saw the same miracle of the spinning sun as he prayed in the Vatican gardens. He took it as a sign that must fulfill the request of Our Lady of Fatima, to consecrate Russia to Her Immaculate Heart, which he did in October 1942.

Many people have seen the spinning sun at Medjigore where Our Lady is reported to have appeared since 1981. People here in our Rosary Group have seen the spinning sun, especially on feast days.

So, Matilda, that is what you, also, saw on Nov. 4th. I hope and pray we are privileged to have another glimpse of this, of this wonderful manifestation in our future meeting, and related blessings from God, and our Blessed Lady.

Hope we meet again soon in the future.

Thank you for your very informative and pleasing letter. God bless you and heal you completely.

From the heart, with love & prayers,

Sister M. Clara

"Write what happened here today in your book, Matilda: it will give inspiration to others."

Sister M. Clara

The Miracle of the Sun[*]

After a downfall of rain, the clouds broke and the sun appeared as an opaque, spinning disk in the sky. It was said to be significantly less bright than normal, and cast multicolored lights across the landscape, the shadows on the landscape, the people, and the surrounding clouds. The sun was reported to have careened towards the earth in a zigzag pattern, frightening some of those present who thought it meant the end of the world. Witnesses reported that the ground and their previously wet clothes became completely dry.

According to witness reports, the alleged miracle of the sun lasted approximately ten minutes. The three shepherd children, in addition to reporting seeing the actions of the sun that day, also reported seeing a panorama of visions, including those of Jesus, the Blessed Virgin Mary, and of Saint Joseph blessing the people.

****
****

Dear Reader, embrace the journey of your life. Live it with love, faith, and the power of prayer.

****
****

---

[*] http://en.wikipedia.org/wiki/The_Miracle_of_the_Sun

Gratitude

My deepest gratitude to Sister Clara, with whom I shared this beautiful, powerful day of blessings and love.

God Bless You.

Heartfelt thanks to the gracious nuns.
Their words rewarded me with wisdom.
Their kindness always gave me joy.

Our Lady of Lourdes Shrine

21281 Chardon Road

Euclid, Ohio 44117-2112

(216)481-8232

www.srstrinity.com